ONE IN A SERIES FROM THE PUBLISHERS OF *PRE-K TODAY*

LEARNING THROUGH PLAY

MATH

A Practical Guide for Teaching Young Children

Written by Sandra Waite - Stupiansky, Ph.D.
and Nicholas G. Stupiansky, Ph.D.

Foreword by Lilian G. Katz, Ph.D.

Contributing Writers:

Ellen Booth Church

Lisa Feeney

Merle Karnes, Ed.D.

Constance Ward

Illustrated by Nicole Rubel

To Nathan and Kristin Stupiansky, our main resources for how young children learn math.
— *Sandra and Nicholas Stupiansky*

Early Childhood Division Vice President and Publisher
Helen Benham

Art Director
Sharon Singer

Production Editor
Katie Lyons

Editors
Nancy-Jo Hereford
Jane Schall

Associate Editor
Ilene S. Rosen

Activity Plans written by
Ellen Booth Church, Lisa Feeney, and Constance Ward

Special thanks to the teachers and children at the SUNY-Plattsburgh Child Care Center, who allowed us to observe their math explorations, and especially to Sally Girard, for all of her helpful comments on the many drafts of the book.

Published by:
Scholastic Inc.
Early Childhood Division
730 Broadway
New York, NY 10003

ISBN # 0-590-49175-X

12, 11, 10, 9, 8, 7, 6, 5, 4, 3   4, 5, 6, 7, 8/9
33

Printed in the U.S.A.
First Scholastic printing, March 1992

CONTENTS

LEARNING AND GROWING WITH MATH

ACTIVITY PLANS FOR TWOS, THREES, FOURS, AND FIVES

Cover Photo: Monkmeyer Press; © Harriet Newman-Brown

> **"A** mathematician, like a poet, ... is a maker of patterns."
>
> **Godfrey Harold Hardy**
> *English Mathematician*

FOREWORD
Talking With Lilian G. Katz

You've spoken and written often about the importance of helping young children acquire "dispositions," as well as knowledge and skills. What are dispositions and why do they matter?

Katz: I call dispositions "habits of mind." Curiosity is a disposition. So is generosity. It's not something you can readily learn, in the way you can learn facts and concepts and skills. Yet children do acquire some dispositions by seeing them modeled. Children are also born with some dispositions that teachers can strengthen to help them learn knowledge and skills.

Can we help young children acquire the disposition to learn math or to be curious about the mathematical relationships in the every-day world?

Katz: Young children are born investigators. They're born with the disposition to learn, to try, to make sense of the world around them, and that certainly includes mathematical relationships. What we as teachers of young children must do is strengthen that natural disposition and guard against damaging it.

How do we strengthen it?

Katz: By giving children ample opportunities to explore freely, to make decisions about what they'll do, and then to evaluate what happens. Teachers are often surprised at how well children can evaluate their own experiences and pinpoint their *own* flaws in reasoning. But that's why encouraging children to talk about their experiences, to talk about the mathematical relationships they see, is so important — as a way to help children verbalize their thinking and identify their own mistakes in logic.

What can damage it?

Katz: Giving young children worksheets instead of offering hands-on experiences. Young children are eager to please, and they'll do the worksheets because we ask them to. But many of them will not be ready and will fail. That's the risk of introducing young children to academic work too soon. If we work at these so-called basic skills too soon and too hard, we may eventually help children to acquire them, but in the process we damage their disposition — their habit of mind — to use those skills.

Considering whether something is developmentally appropriate means not only worrying about what children do today, but also about the long-term consequences. It's not much use having the skills to read or to work with numbers by the elementary years if you really feel that the minute you get out of a classroom, you won't ever read or won't ever do math again.

So it is critical to develop both skills and the disposition to use them?

Katz: Absolutely. The major responsibility of teachers at every level is to figure out how to help children acquire the skills they need, and, at the same time, to strengthen their disposition to use those skills. At the early childhood level, it involves engaging children in experiences that let them investigate and explore, confirming for them that these skills are not mindless, that they are worth doing and thinking about.

You advocate a project approach to learning as one way to engage children in worthwhile activities. How does math fit into this approach?

Katz: It fits in very easily. A project by definition is an in-depth study of a topic or theme that interests children, such as learning about the bus that brings us to preschool. A project connects many areas of the curriculum in a coherent way. And just about any kind of project a group might do — like building a house or learning about the hospital — will have some math connection, some reason to quantify or to measure. While the teacher guides the project, much of the planning and all of the making and creating and active learning are done by the children. So a project approach is a good way to help children engage in math learning in an exciting and meaningful context.

> *Young children are born investigators. It's our job to strengthen that disposition.*

Lilian G. Katz, Ph.D., is professor of early childhood education at the University of Illinois at Urbana-Champaign. Dr. Katz is an internationally known author, lecturer, and researcher on the education of young children. She is also integrally involved with the National Association for the Education of Young Children. Her most recent book is Engaging Children's Minds: The Project Approach, *co-authored with Sylvia C. Chard (Ablex, 1991).*

YOUR ROLE
IN FOSTERING
MATH LEARNING

Math learning happens naturally as children play. Young children discover, test, and apply math concepts naturally every day, in just about everything they do. Some kinds of math learning seem obvious, such as when you count with four-year-old Sheila to see how many blocks are in her tower or when five-year-old Enrico, in answer to a question about how old he is, holds up five fingers. But children are also "doing math" as they discuss whose cup is biggest or which bucket holds the most sand. They are developing problem-solving skills by working through playtime dilemmas, such as deciding which size block will make the best roof for a building.

Your role in fostering math learning is to build on children's natural curiosity about shapes, sizes, amounts, and other fundamentals of math. This book will offer plenty of help in integrating experiences with math into children's everyday play. But remember that you are the one who will make it work. Your excitement and interest in children's inquiries will encourage them to talk through their discoveries. Your acceptance of their math reasoning, even when it may seem "wrong" or illogical, will give them the confidence to keep thinking, questioning, and sharing.

MUST YOU BE A MATH WHIZ YOURSELF?

If you've been reading this and thinking, "Oh, but I'm no good in math," you're not alone. For many intelligent and able adults, the word "math" triggers feelings of inadequacy or "math anxiety" — a general feeling of not being comfortable with or competent in math. Most often, these feelings stem from childhood experiences with math that placed too much emphasis on getting correct answers, when the process of finding the answers was not fully understood.

How can you fight feelings of math anxiety when working with young children? First, remember that you won't ever — and should never — "teach" number tables, addition and subtraction, or other types of formal math learning to young children. They are far from developmentally ready to acquire those kinds of math skills.

What young math thinkers need most is an adult who fosters their interest in math. They need someone who encourages them to test their ideas and to keep sharing their reasoning with the confidence and assurance that it will be accepted, no matter what! Children don't need you to know all the answers. In fact, it's often better if you don't, because then teacher and children can enjoy the process of learning and discovering math together.

PREVENTING MATH ANXIETY FROM THE START

Children, too, can develop math anxiety. When we show by our concern with "right" answers that we're disappointed in the way children are thinking, we aid in developing a sense of inadequacy. Take four-year-old Casey, who happily declares that she traded her two dimes for four pennies and now feels much richer. If we quickly point out her mistake, she may begin to doubt her own perceptions of what is so obvious to her — pennies are bigger than dimes and four is more than two. Both observations are correct, and before long Casey will learn the value of various coins. But her belief in herself as a capable math thinker will be under-

mined if we dwell on what she doesn't know, rather than on what she does.

Sometimes, in our vigor to "teach" children math, we rush them along before they are ready. We may ask children to copy numerals that symbolize concepts they do not understand. A child who can recognize a "6" might still think, "Five elephants is more than six ants." This child needs more concrete experiences with groups of five and six objects.

Remember that young children need time to explore and discover math concepts on their own. In a supportive, non-judgmental environment, they become confident learners who see math as a natural and valuable part of everyday activities. And the best way to develop positive attitudes toward and solid aptitude for math is through the very experiences that early childhood professionals are best at guiding — open-ended, child-directed play!

HELPING CHILDREN LEARN MATH NATURALLY, THROUGH PLAY

As children touch, pour, shape, and order materials around them, they discover relationships among objects. Juan, for example, finds that one car goes faster than another down the block ramp. He has a new way of identifying the cars as the "fast red car" and the "faster yellow car." Lydia discovers that when she plunges the big plastic jug down into the water table, it fills with water. Now it's so heavy she can hardly lift it. That never happens with the small jar. Lydia has discovered a new way of comparing.

Each new discovery about the physical world, and the thinking that accompanies these discoveries, lays the foundation for later mathematical learning. When Juan reaches elementary school, his preschool experiences will prepare him for learning to calculate differences in distance and speed. Lydia's early discoveries will give her a concrete understanding of how to measure volume.

AGES & STAGES
IN MATH LEARNING

Naturally, children don't think or act alike as math learners. Their age and developmental levels play a big role in determining what math skills they're able to master and what concepts they understand. These guidelines can help prepare you for the kinds of math learning you may see in children ages two to five.

TWO-YEAR-OLDS MAY:
- Count two or three objects.
- Begin to use relationship words such as "more juice," "little baby," or "very tired."
- Build with blocks, by stacking and then toppling them.
- Recognize a circle and other very simple geometric shapes.

THREE-YEAR-OLDS MAY:
- Count three or four objects by pointing at them. If, after the child counts, you ask how many objects there are, most three-year-olds will need to count all over again.
- When counting more than five objects, threes often count some objects twice and skip over others. Getting a different total each time they count the same group of objects doesn't bother them.
- Use words that imply size and quantity relationships: "Mom is the biggest." "I have more raisins than you."
- Begin to use shape to help them place puzzle pieces.

FOUR-YEAR-OLDS MAY:
- Spontaneously use math to solve real-life problems: "There are four people at my party, so I need four cups."

- Begin to develop one-to-one correspondence with small groups: one cup for each person; one chair for each person.
- Begin to see and name patterns around them: circle, circle, square; red, blue, red, blue.
- Estimate quantities randomly. The pumpkin may weigh one pound or one thousand pounds to a four-year-old.
- Sort objects by classifying. Fours sort by one characteristic at a time, such as size, color, or shape.

FIVE-YEAR-OLDS MAY:

- Count objects up to 10 with few mistakes.
- Recognize more complex patterns: little, medium, bigger, medium, little; "My shirt has green-blue-yellow, green-blue-yellow stripes."
- Enjoy beginning games that involve moving markers around a board a certain number of spaces or to a particular color.
- Use relationship words — sometimes invented by them — that demonstrate a recognition of finer grades of differences: "I have the mostest cookies. You have the next mostest."
- Solve multi-piece puzzles by recognizing geometric shapes and fine details.
- Sequence five or more objects in order by size or using other physical differences.
- Classify objects into sets, such as grouping fruits by color. Fives begin to see that the same group of objects can be sorted many different ways, such as fruits that are smooth and shiny, bumpy, squishy, or round.
- Count a small group of objects and recall how many are in the group when asked several seconds later.
- Confuse sets within sets, such as whether there are more girls or more children in the room. If there are more girls than boys, fives may still say that there are more girls than children.

(Coincidentally, elementary educators — taking the lead from their early childhood colleagues — increasingly recognize the value of hands-on math learning for older children, too!)

Learning to be a math thinker also involves using math to solve problems, and the everyday life of preschool offers an endless array. Determining how many sandwiches to make for the picnic lunch or how many buckets of sand are needed to fill the sandbox are real challenges — problems children can solve together or on their own.

FOLLOWING THE CHILD'S LEAD

As we observe children exploring math concepts through play, the message we communicate through our questions and responses should be, "Tell me what you think," and not, "Give me the right answer." If we watch closely and listen uncritically, young children will tell us much about how they think. If we ask questions that have many possible responses, they'll amaze us with the range and creativity of the answers they offer!

Here is a summary of tips to keep in mind as you watch for and encourage math experiences through everyday play:

- *"Look at that!"* Encourage children to be aware of and curious about objects, actions, and events around them that contribute to math learning. Point out patterns in the floor tiles, the sizes of trees on the playground, and the shapes of windows in buildings you pass on daily walks. Use words that describe the relationships among objects and events: "The snail moves across the sidewalk so slowly; the turtle moves a little quicker." "I want a half of a sandwich because I am not very hungry today."

- *"I can touch that!"* Provide concrete math materials that are child-friendly and that can be manipulated in many ways, such as buttons that can be sorted by size, color, or number of holes; and containers of many sizes that can be filled, spilled, and refilled. Remember, too, that while you'll want to set up a math-manipulatives center in your room, where children know they will find materials from puzzles to pattern blocks, items to encourage math learning should be part of every activity setting, indoors and out. (For guidance on setting up a math center and for inte-

Photo: Kate Connell

grating math activities into other areas, see "Setting Up for Math Learning," pages 22-29.)

■ *"Can you show me how to write my phone number?"* Wait until children show a need or an interest in number symbols before introducing them, then choose numerals that have meaning for individuals, such as their ages or phone numbers. Remember that learning number symbols is not nearly as important as understanding the concepts that they represent.

■ *"You can have a half, Terry can have a half, and I can have a half."* Encourage children to talk about number concepts without fear of being wrong. Children will make many incorrect statements in the process of learning math, just as they do when learning to talk. Correcting them may discourage children from offering their own solutions. If they think that three people can each have half of the same sandwich, they are using the wrong term, but they have the right idea of half being a fraction of a whole.

■ *"She has more applesauce than I have!"* Solving real-life problems provides the opportunity for children to apply mathematical reasoning in meaningful ways. Try the children's solutions to see what works. Spoon out the applesauce according to their directions — even if you have to do it several times before everyone is happy. Remember, no solution is a bad solution.

■ *"Look, I can make a '4'!"* As adults, we generally view math as an exercise of the mind — the skill we use to balance our checkbook. But that's only part of the equation for preschoolers. The young child who makes a "4" is exercising fine-motor skills, too. Math stretches young children cognitively, but it also enhances every other area of the whole child. It challenges the child's creative-thinking skills. It can be a physical activity that develops fine- and gross-motor skills. Whether it's a pair solving a puzzle together or a foursome

sharing an apple among them, math experiences help hone essential social skills. And success as a math thinker helps the child reach emotional milestones, like developing self-confidence. The chart on pages 18-21, "Learning and Growing With Math," outlines in detail how each area of a child's development is challenged and refined through everyday math discoveries.

MATH IS A WAY OF THINKING

Learning math involves so much more than rote counting or tracing numerals. The section that follows, "Hands-On Skills for Young Math Thinkers," identifies important math skills and concepts that young children can learn through play. But essentially, math also involves learning to think in a logical way. Here we will fail if we try to "teach" preschool children to reason logically, because, developmentally, they're not ready. They may leave our programs able to recognize shapes and patterns, to order objects by size, or to understand one-to-one correspondence. But they won't leave as logical thinkers.

It takes time for children to acquire logic and reasoning skills. As they grow and mature, and as they experience opportunities to discover and apply math concepts in ways that are meaningful to them and to test their reasoning to see if it holds, their thinking naturally becomes more logical. But children have to go through stages of thinking illogically before they arrive at the logical means adults use to order and make predictions about the world.

So we're back to our most important role in fostering math learning — to provide the stimulation and encouragement to help children develop and practice their own thinking, to learn math by DOING math, to make mistakes, and, in time, to learn from them. When we fulfill this role, we help children take giant steps toward becoming competent, confident math thinkers!

HANDS – ON SKILLS
FOR YOUNG MATH THINKERS

Just as children learn to crawl before they walk or scribble before they write, they learn to think about math by first developing some of the key foundation skills.

Like the process skills in science that help children learn more about their world — observing, classifying, predicting, etc. — math process skills help children begin to understand the mathematical relationships in the world around them. These skills include the following: patterning, sorting and classifying, ordering and seriating, beginning number concepts, problem solving, measuring and estimating, and visual/spatial awareness.

Naturally, children do not acquire these skills overnight. They take many years to develop fully, in some cases long into the elementary years. And children develop them at different rates, becoming adept to different degrees. You know that some adults are better problem solvers, while others are quicker to recognize a pattern or to estimate an amount or a measurement. Children, too, are often better at some math processes than others, and that's to be expected and accepted. But your role is still to provide a range of activities that will help all of your children gain experience with all of these foundation skills.

Most important, remember that these skills are best developed in natural, meaningful settings, using concrete materials that children manipulate and explore on their own. These are not skills to "teach." They're skills for children to discover and refine through everyday play. By providing children with the kinds of materials that encourage them to sort and classify, for example, or to naturally order a set of objects from biggest to smallest, you'll encourage them to use and enhance these skills.

This section will help you provide the materials, setting, and guidance to promote understanding of these seven "themes" in math learning. Use these pages to help you plan for the kinds of experiences that give young children the best possible math beginnings.

PATTERNING

A pattern is a sequence of colors, shapes, objects, sounds, or movements that repeats again and again and again. Children explore patterns in different play settings all the time. Jesse, for example, notices that the beads in the dress-up necklace she's wearing are arranged red/blue/yellow, red/blue/yellow. Marsha uses green and blue paint at the easel to imitate the green/blue/green/blue stripes on her pants. As Nathan places triangle/square/triangle/square in a line across the floor of the math-manipulatives center, he boasts that it's the longest line of shapes in the world. In his excitement, Nathan has created a pattern!

■ Where do we find patterns in our world? Patterns are everywhere. Visual patterns appear in the bricks in the sidewalk, the designs on the rug, and the checks on shirts and sweaters. Auditory patterns are found in the melodies of music, rhythms of clapping games, and repetitive language or sounds of predictable stories and fingerplays. Physical patterns are embedded in dance and exercise sequences.

■ What are different activities related to patterning? The simplest activity for children is identifying an existing pattern, such as when Jesse recognizes that the beads in the necklace are arranged in a color sequence of red/blue/yellow.

Next in difficulty is matching patterns. For example, Jesse might find a dress-up shirt with the same color pattern of red/blue/yellow.

The next step in advancing patterning skills is being able to copy a pattern. Marsha does that when she makes green and blue stripes on her paper, to match the green and blue stripes on her pants.

A more difficult skill is extending an existing pattern. You begin a pattern of red circle/green rectangle using shape blocks. Nathan sees your pattern and continues positioning red circles and green rectangles.

The most difficult patterning skill is creating a new pattern, such as Nathan's own shape sequence of triangle/square/triangle/square.

However, children don't always acquire patterning skills in this order. Some will be able to create their own patterns but will have great difficulty extending an existing pattern. That's why it's so important to observe children as they use manipulatives, to get a sense of what skills they are strong in and which they find more difficult.

■ Why is patterning important? Identifying and creating patterns helps children see relationships between and among things and expands their understanding of similarities and differences. Working with patterns helps children develop important thinking skills, such as learning to analyze (to see the parts of a whole), as well as to synthesize (to see how parts form a whole). Patterning also helps children develop math-language skills as they talk about patterns they observe or create.

■ **What hands-on materials can be used in patterning activities?** Beads and colored cubes or blocks are popular patterning materials, but just about any material that can be arranged in recurring patterns and that children can explore and experiment with safely is fine.

REMEMBER
■ Start with very simple two-element patterns (AB) before exploring with more difficult three-or-more-element patterns (ABC, AAB, AABB).
■ Include auditory patterns in the form of clapping games, fingerplays, stories with repetitive words, as well as movement patterns. However, children will find it easier to learn patterning skills by experimenting with physical materials, so provide lots of manipulatives, too.
■ Promote patterning activities at each level of difficulty —identifying, matching, copying, extending, and creating patterns.

SORTING AND CLASSIFYING

Sorting and classifying objects by common qualities is one of the most familiar math activities at any age. You see children sorting and classifying all the time! In the math-manipulatives center, Jamie and Maria empty a container of buttons on the floor. Jamie searches for all the black buttons and puts them in one pile, as Maria looks for buttons that are more square than round.

Meanwhile, in the art area, Linda, Emile, and José are cutting out pictures of things with wheels to paste on poster paper. When asked, they're happy to explain that the car, bike, truck, and doll carriage they've pictured so far belong together because they all have wheels. Children first learn to sort and classify objects by shape, then by color, then by size.

Why are sorting and classifying important? Classification activities sharpen observation skills as children look for likenesses and differences. And as children become more adept at comparing familiar objects, they're more able to compare sets of objects that represent different numbers. Classifying also helps children make sense of their surroundings. They see there is an organization to the world — that different things belong together in groups.

How can you encourage sorting and classifying activities? Opportunities for sorting and classifying occur naturally throughout your day. Cleanup time is one of the most obvious: blocks are sorted by size or shape for storing on shelves. Clothing and accessories are sorted and classified by type in the dramatic-play area. Markers are sorted by color for storage.

The kinds of materials you provide in different play areas will encourage more experiences with classifying. Just about any collection of objects, from bottle caps in the manipulatives center to shoes in the pretend shoe store, can be sorted and classified by some common characteristic. Include an array of heavy and light objects at the water table and you're sure to see children classifying items by those that float and those that sink.

REMEMBER
■ Children often think of ways to classify that adults don't. Always ask a child to tell you about how he or she sorted a group of objects. You'll discover a lot about children's thinking and creativity.
■ The scheme a child uses to classify objects is more important than the physical sorting. He may miss an object or two, and that's okay. What matters is what quality the child thinks the objects share in common.
■ Children will first sort and classify by looking at only one quality — such as objects that are red and those that are not red; or objects that are big and objects that are little. As children become more competent at sorting and

MAKING TIME CONCEPTS MEANINGFUL

Children are naturally curious about time. They ask how long until snack, how long until story, how long until it's time to go home, and even how long until they can come back. But curiosity about time doesn't mean that children are ready to tell time using clocks or to recognize the passing of time using calendars.

Because time is a very abstract concept, it takes many years, generally well into the primary grades, before children are ready to learn to tell time using a standard clock. Once they recognize numerals, children may be able to read a digitized clock or watch. But unless they have internalized what numbers mean, 5:15 is just a five and a one and five, with some funny dots in between.

As well, a child needs an understanding of number to see meaning in a date such as October 5. And children who still confuse yesterday and tomorrow are not ready to use calendars to represent dates for times in the past or future.

classifying, they're more able to sort by more than one quality, such as fruits that are red and also shiny.

ORDERING AND SERIATING

Linda is busy arranging the stuffed animals in the dramatic-play area from smallest to largest. Niko and Kris are using a wooden ramp to see which toy car is fastest and which is slowest. Matthew is arranging the crayons he may use in his picture from the lightest color to the darkest.

What do these activities have in common? All are a type of ordering activity called seriation.

■ **What is seriation?** Seriation involves identifying differences between objects and arranging or ordering the objects according to those differences. In the process of ordering objects by size or speed or brightness of color, children develop ways of thinking about a group of objects. Thus, Niko and Kris learn from their explorations that all of the cars they test will move, but some will move faster than others. When they transfer that understanding to the real world, they'll recognize that objects which move don't all move at the same speed. Some move faster than others. They can order those objects, too, from slowest to fastest, or fastest to slowest.

■ **Why are ordering and seriating important math skills?** Seriation is basic to understanding much about the world around us — that even objects that are classified together are different by degrees.

Seriation is also basic to understanding the meaning and order of numbers. Children begin ordering objects by physical characteristics, such as size, texture, color, and speed; but gradually they progress to ordering by quantity. As children recognize that two is one more than one and that three is one more than two, the order of the numbers — one, two, three, four — takes on real meaning for them.

■ **What kinds of materials encourage seriating activities?** Any objects that can be ordered make good seriating materials. Cups filled with different amounts of water can be ordered from most full to least full. Paint-chip samples, crayons and markers, and fabric remnants can be ordered by color hue. Measuring cups, bottles, and other containers can be ordered by size. Carpet squares can be ordered by texture, such as softest to least soft. And, of course, people can be ordered by height, weight, age, and by many other characteristics, too.

REMEMBER

■ Start with no more than three objects when first introducing children to seriating activities. Encourage the child to compare two objects and put them in order, then to compare the third object to the first two. As children's seriating skills build, increase the number of objects they order to four or more.

■ As with classifying and sorting activities, always ask a child to tell you how he or she ordered a set of objects. Children may see differences that adults don't.

■ Seriating activities encourage the use of comparative language. Model these words by using terms such as *smaller*, *lighter*, *taller*, *younger*, and *older* as you discuss order together.

■ With time and experience, children will start to recognize that the same group of objects can be ordered in more than one way — from largest to smallest and smallest to largest.

BEGINNING NUMBER CONCEPTS

Ashley is busy placing one car in each parking place. Michael is helping to set the table for snack, trying to figure out how many cups and napkins are needed. Brent and Natasha are arguing over who has collected more acorns on the playground. What is the common theme? Children's understanding of number is evident in each of these everyday experiences.

Building on what children know helps them understand future and past. Children can grasp that tomorrow is when they wake up the next time. They can understand yesterday in terms of events they enjoyed, such as going to the pumpkin farm. Explaining that tomorrow is the twelfth if today is the eleventh, or that yesterday was October 28, will have little or no relevance to a young child. And, chances are, you will only get a quizzical look and the question repeated: "But just when is tomorrow?"

So what is the best way to introduce the concept of time with young children? Start with what they understand. Set up a regular schedule, so children know the main sequence of activities — and what to expect next — during the day. Reminding a child that outdoor time will come after lunch has much more meaning than telling the child that outdoor time is at one o'clock. Yet, you are still helping children begin to recognize that a day is ordered in some way. Right now, it's ordered for children in terms of events. Eventually, they'll understand that a day is also ordered by hours; that days order a week; that weeks order a month; that months order a year.

■ **What skills are considered "beginning number concepts?"** Number concepts involve thinking about "how many" or "how much." Beginning number concepts include counting, one-to-one correspondence, and most important, understanding the meaning of number.

Learning the meaning of number, also called "conservation of number," is truly a foundation skill, for a child's work with numbers throughout school depends on this understanding. It involves recognizing that a number does not change — that the five dots on the face of a number cube represent the same amount as five fingers on a hand, or five points on a star, or five boxcars on a train. This understanding only develops with time, and with repeated opportunities to work with groups of objects and compare amounts. By contrast, a young child who has not developed conservation of number might say, "Five elephants is more than five ants," because elephants are so much bigger than ants.

Counting involves learning the sequence of number names, then using those numbers to identify quantities of objects. But counting is a tricky skill to evaluate, because a child may be able to say number words and still not associate numbers with the concept of "how many." To use number words to count groups of objects and know how many acorns she has, for example, a child must both know the sequence of the numbers and know what those numbers represent.

One-to-one correspondence involves matching objects from one group with objects from another to determine if the groups have an equal number of objects. Matching naturally leads to thinking about greater than, less than, and equal to, more key math terms and understandings. As children solve real problems, such as making sure each has a carpet square to sit on or each doctor has a doll to care for, they employ one-to-one correspondence in meaningful ways.

■ **What is the difference between numbers and numerals?** A numeral is a symbol — "5." A number is the idea of what "five" really means. Children learn numerals in three ways. They say them orally ("four"), they learn the symbol (4), and they learn the written word (*four*). Children do need to learn numerals, but being able to write a "4" or pick out the "4" on a page is not as important as understanding the meaning of "four."

■ **What's the best way for children to learn number concepts?** Number concepts are complex and not easy for children to learn. Pictures on worksheets or objects to count, unconnected to anything else, do not enhance this learning process. Instead, children need a variety of meaningful experiences with number concepts — experiences like counting to see if we have 12 plates and 12 napkins for the group, then using one-to-one correspondence to give one plate and one napkin to each child. As children become more able to classify and to group objects, they learn from experience that a group of five objects is always more than a group of four objects, even if the four objects happen to be elephants and the five objects are ants.

REMEMBER

■ Acquiring number concepts is a gradual process. As children manipulate objects, using language to explain their thinking, they begin to construct number meanings.

■ Children often use trial and error in developing skills in counting and one-to-one correspondence. For example, it's common to see a young child in the housekeeping corner make many trips to the cupboard, getting one cup at a time, until he or she has enough cups for all of the dolls at the tea party. (For more guidance on ages and stages and number skills, see the sidebar on pages 7-8.)

■ Rhymes, fingerplays, and number songs are appropriate ways to reinforce the sequence of numbers. Just remember that memorizing number words is more a language skill than a skill that teaches number meaning.

PROBLEM SOLVING

Problem solving is applying math in workable ways. Problems involving the use of math skills and concepts happen everywhere: snacktime, circle time, in the block corner, at the water table, outside on the playground, etc.

For instance, when Meagan, Jimmy, and Paula try to figure out how to share the five dolls in the dramatic-play area equally among them, that's problem solving. When Amanda and Teri try to figure out how many more Lincoln Logs it will take to complete the fence for their corral, that's also problem solving. And when Larry builds a block bridge — but it keeps falling down — he uses problem-solving skills, even if he's not immediately successful, in pinpointing what's wrong and how to fix it.

■ **What's the value of problem-solving activities?** Problem solving is a process that provides a context for applying many math skills and concepts. When the math connections to problem situations are clear, the math skills and concepts children draw on to find workable solutions are more meaningful to them. They may learn through matching dolls to children that three children and five dolls are unequal groups and cannot be "shared equally" — without finding a very creative solution. They may employ measuring skills to figure out how many more Lincoln Logs they need. Or they may learn some important lessons about which length or shape block is needed to build a sturdy bridge. Most important, they learn that math has real value. They can use math skills and concepts to make their everyday lives easier!

Problem-solving experiences also offer children opportunities to share their thinking and ideas with other children. And as children experience success in solving problems, they gain confidence in their abilities.

■ **How can you encourage math problem solving?** First and foremost, don't be too quick to solve problems for children. Encourage them to explore and investigate on their own. Problem situations will arise all the time. Use open-ended questions — such as "How can you find out if there are more dolls or more children?" — to urge children to think about ways to approach a problem. And provide lots of encouragement to help children keep trying ideas until they find a solution they're satisfied with.

REMEMBER
■ Actively listen to and accept children's ideas and responses. Communicate that there are many ways of doing the same thing.
■ Encourage risk-taking. Children will approach problem situations with excitement in an atmosphere where they do not fear failure.
■ Encourage children to help one another solve problems by sharing ideas and possible solutions.

MEASURING AND ESTIMATING

Sean is filling cups with sand, then dumping them into the back of the dump truck. You hear him wonder aloud how many more cups before the truck is full. Meanwhile, Miguel is busy seeing how many orange rods fit across the tabletop when lined up end to end. Sara is doing the same thing, using the purple rods that are shorter in length. As Miguel finishes, Sara estimates that she's almost finished, too — about two more purple rods are all she needs.

What math skills are these children using? Of course, they're measuring and estimating.

■ **What is measuring — and how do children learn to measure?** Measuring involves determining amounts. Young children are exposed to many kinds of measuring devices, even if they can't use and understand each one. Clocks measure time, thermometers measure temperature, special spoons and cups measure quantity, rulers measure length, and scales measure weight.

As adults, we tend to think of measurement in terms of rulers and scales. But a unit of measure such as an inch is an abstract concept to a young child. Children are naturally curious about how big or heavy something is or which has more or less. They draw on skills of classification and comparison, and on their emerging understanding of what numbers mean, as they learn to measure. So anything that helps them make these comparisons in ways that make sense to them is a good measuring material.

■ **What is estimating, and what is its value?** Estimating involves using numbers to make a guess or a prediction. Estimating helps to make math a more usable skill in everyday life. While sometimes an exact answer is necessary, sometimes an approximation is all that's needed.

It takes practice to become good at estimating, so starting children at a young age will help them become more able estimators throughout life. Opportunities for estimating occur naturally — when measuring, counting, sharing materials or snacks. For example, before distributing crackers at snacktime, show children the whole box and ask them to estimate how many crackers there are. Count together to check the accuracy of your estimates. With experience, children will become better at making close estimates.

REMEMBER

■ Use concrete, meaningful materials for beginning measuring and estimating activities. The number of footsteps to get from one end of the room to the other, the number of hand widths to cross a tabletop, and the number of cups of water to equal the weight of the rock are all examples.

■ Children need frequent practice with these skills, preferably as part of problem-solving activities. They should always be active measurers and estimators, not passive observers.

■ Model words that signal estimates, such as *about*, *a little more/less than*, *near*, and *between*.

VISUAL/SPATIAL SKILLS

Tara is stretching a rubber band around the pegs of a geoboard, discov-

MATH FOR
MIXED-AGE GROUPS

Helping children recognize how math fits into daily life can be even easier to accomplish in the setting of a family day-care home. After all, there are so many real-life activities going on that incorporate math. Measuring ingredients as you prepare meals together, counting out the plates and spoons as children set the table, and asking them to sort the silverware after the dishes are done, are just a few of the many ways you can bring in math skills and concepts through everyday experiences. And then there are those special activities, such as inviting children to help you measure a plot of ground outdoors for a garden, that enhance math thinking in memorable ways.

Of course, your special challenge as a family day-care provider is working with a group of children who may range considerably in age and developmental levels. These tips can help. Review them for guidance in making the most of the math connections in your home setting, in ways that are appropriate for each of the children you care for.

■ *Choose materials that can be used at different levels.* As you select manipulative materials, consider ways those same items could be used by children of different ages. For example, counters that are too big to swallow but interesting to older preschoolers can be stacked or lined up in a row by a two-year-old, while a four- or five-year-old will count, sort, and match them one to one. Plastic containers of all sizes and shapes make wonderful items for any age to explore with in the sandbox or in a tub of water.

■ *Plan for safety.* Opt first for manipulatives that are large

ering what types of shapes she can make. Timmy is working with pattern blocks, making sunbursts and other designs. Jill is trying to build a house out of blocks just like the house Lisa has built on the other side of the block area. All of these activities involve visual/spatial skills.

■ **What are visual/spatial skills?**
Spatial sense is an intuitive feel for one's surroundings and the objects in them. To develop spatial sense, children need many experiences with geometric relationships they see — from recognizing shapes and sizes to understanding positions and directions like *above*, *below*, *right*, and *left*.

■ **Why are these skills important?**
Our understanding of what we see often depends on our perspective. An object can look very different when viewed from above or below, or from the right or the left.

For beginning learners, a knowledge of informal geometry is needed to learn to read and write letters and numerals. Visual-discrimination skills and motor skills are also related to the development of visual/spatial skills.

■ **How are visual/spatial skills developed?** Activities that involve hands-on exploration with physical materials and everyday objects set the stage for learning spatial skills. Children who are able to visualize, draw, and compare shapes in various positions are developing spatial skills.

Movement activities help children acquire spatial understanding by feeling what it's like to be *above* or *below* or *over* or *under* or *in between*. Emphasize these spatial terms as you enjoy games and activities that incorporate them.

REMEMBER
■ Young children should focus on simple shapes — circles, squares, and triangles. Don't try to introduce more complex, many-sided shapes.
■ Children need opportunities to explore the properties of shapes, to compare them, and to see how some are related (such as squares and triangles or ovals and circles). Look for natural ways to build in these experiences, such as by finding shapes in nature.

You can be sure children will develop a foundation for mathematical reasoning as they practice these seven skills.

and easily handled by fingers of all sizes, such as large counting cubes or shape blocks. If you do offer small manipulatives to older preschoolers — such as your button collection to sort, classify, count, and form patterns with — remember that these items can easily end up in the mouths of toddlers. Engage younger children in a separate activity when older preschoolers are playing with these manipulatives. Teach older ones the importance of picking up carefully when they finish play, then store the items well out of the reach of younger children.

■ *Ask open-ended questions to encourage responses on many levels.* Questions with many possible responses — the kind that ask how and why and what do you think — tell children that you're not looking for a "right answer." When children know that, they feel freer to explore and to use materials in their own ways — in the ways they're capable of for their age — and to share their thinking with you. In turn, listening to children's thought processes can help you extend their math explorations with another question or with a new experience.

■ *Encourage multiage interactions.* As children play togeth-er, older children will naturally model more complex math thinking. For instance, when children engage in pretend play, older preschoolers may demonstrate one-to-one correspondence for younger children as they make sure each person at the teddy bear's birthday party has a plate, fork, and spoon. Likewise, as children play together with blocks, older preschoolers may model using geometry and measurement to form more complex structures.

Both ages gain from such interactions. Younger children are helped to advance in their own math skills. And as older children explain what they're doing to their younger peers, they verbalize their math thinking. This helps them confirm their own logic or recognize flaws in their reasoning.

■ *Hold age-appropriate expectations for each child.* A young child who's just learning to count to three will be frustrated if asked to count sets of more than three objects. On the other hand, an older preschooler who can count to 10 is likely to greet a request to count three books with, "That's easy!" Observe what each child is able to do and set your expectations accordingly, so that children are challenged but not discouraged in their efforts to learn math.

LEARNING AND GROWING

More than many other areas of the early childhood curriculum, we tend to think of math as a cognitive experience. Yet, as this four-page chart shows, math activities develop the whole child — socially, emotionally, creatively, and physically — as well as intellectually. So when children are busy actively learning math concepts, they're also learning so much more!

Under each area of development, you'll find key skills or concepts that math activities can enhance or refine. Reproduce this chart to help staff members and parents understand and appreciate the important strengths of math learning.

Here's how to follow the chart. Each entry begins with a description of the skill or concept and how it develops as children learn to think mathematically. "Ways to Assist" are suggestions you can use to promote further development. "Developmental Considerations" are guidelines to help you know what to expect from younger children (twos and threes) and from older preschoolers (fours and fives). Naturally, behavior varies greatly at all ages, so view these as guidelines only.

WITH MATH

SOCIAL & EMOTIONAL DEVELOPMENT

DEVELOPING SELF-CONFIDENCE

When children act on their own ideas, exploring math without fear of failure, self-confidence grows. And when children feel confident as math thinkers, their understanding of math concepts blossoms!

Ways to Assist

■ Encourage and support children's attempts at math reasoning. When Bethany counts her fingers and gets five one time and four the next, it shows she needs more time to develop one-to-one correspondence. Rather than correct her and possibly make her feel she has done something wrong, ask open-ended questions with many possible responses. When children suspect you're looking for a "right" answer, they may feel a loss of confidence, especially if they don't know what that answer is.

Accept children's responses, even if they seem illogical; then ask for their reasoning. When Juan places a banana with strawberries and cherries, he may be grouping fruits by ones he likes, not by color.

Developmental Considerations

■ Twos and threes generally approach new situations with curiosity and confidence. When nurtured, these traits help them tackle everyday math problems.

■ Fours and fives are more aware that there can be right and wrong ways to do things. They need an environment in which they feel free to test ideas without fear of judgment or failure.

COOPERATING & SHARING

As children work together and share materials, they challenge and encourage one another in exciting ways. As they put together a puzzle, they may discuss where each piece can go and whether it fits. As they divvy up play clay, they redivide until everyone has the same amount. Children who are at a more advanced developmental stage often provide the stimulation to help peers move to the next level of thinking.

Ways to Assist

■ Provide opportunities for children to learn together by planning for small groups in your math-manipulatives center.

■ Offer ample amounts of even a limited variety of materials, so children focus more on creating together than on getting control of scarce resources.

■ Encourage children to learn from one another and to solve problems together. When Morgan asks, "Which glass has more milk in it?" say, "Ask Megan what she thinks. She's having milk, too."

Developmental Considerations

■ Younger children are just developing social and language skills. They tend to play alongside, rather than with, others. Remember that they may not be ready to share.

■ Older children communicate more easily as they play and are learning to cooperate and share. Their tendency to compare creations — "My rocket is taller." — makes math learning a natural extension.

CREATIVE DEVELOPMENT

USING CREATIVE THINKING

Advances in mathematics have often been made by individuals who found new ways of thinking about familiar problems. Children need opportunities to try new ways of thinking and problem solving, too. When you create an environment that encourages children to explore math in their own ways, you nurture creative thinking.

Ways to Assist

■ Ask questions with many possible answers: "I wonder how many ways you could build a bridge with this set of blocks?"

■ Pose questions you don't know the answer to, then explore together. "I wonder if this pumpkin weighs more than these apples? How can we find out?"

■ Show by your acceptance of and joy in diversity that there are many ways to do the same thing.

■ Show that you value children's creativity. As they begin to develop number sense, let them choose four objects to draw, instead of coloring four predrawn ducks on a reproducible sheet.

Developmental Considerations

■ Twos and threes often assert their newfound independence by wanting to solve problems in their own ways. Nurture this striving for autonomy. It can lead to creative, divergent thinking.

■ Fours and fives vary in their eagerness to come up with new ideas. But when they feel their ideas are valued, they're more apt to develop their creativity.

LEARNING AND GROWING

FINE-MOTOR SKILLS

As young children manipulate materials that help develop math concepts, such as puzzles, unit blocks, and objects for sorting and counting, they also strengthen finger and hand muscles. And, as fine-motor skills develop, children gain the control to write numerals when they're ready in mind and body.

Ways to Assist
■ Provide ample opportunities for children to work with manipulative materials, such as pegboards, connecting toys, buttons, clay, sand, and water.
■ Make cleanup a time to work on fine-motor skills, too. Matching blocks to silhouettes on shelves and hanging measuring cups on designated pegs help children develop hand and finger control.
■ Let children help with daily tasks that involve fine-motor movements, such as pouring juice for snack and putting books on library shelves. These jobs also involve measuring and classifying, key math skills.

Developmental Considerations
■ Fine-motor skills take most of the early childhood years to develop. Twos and threes need many opportunities to practice in a patient environment where it's okay if little fingers drop, spill, or knock things over.
■ Fours and fives vary greatly in fine-motor skills. Tasks that are low-risk, such as using scissors to cut paper randomly, rather than following pre-drawn lines, help each refine fine-motor skills at his or her own pace.

GROSS-MOTOR SKILLS

Combining math and gross-motor movements is a great way to help young children see math as an active area of learning. Encourage this understanding with such exercises as whole-body measuring, running and jumping various distances, and throwing balls of various sizes.

Ways to Assist
■ Encourage active play with a variety of materials such as ramps, slides, ladders of different inclines, and climbing surfaces of different heights. A set of objects that vary in one way, such as height, helps children compare relationships, an important math skill.
■ Plan for directed activities that let children use their bodies to try out math skills. A "Simon Says" game for younger children could test spatial awareness: "reach up high"; "squat down low." Older children can follow more complex directions: "jump up and down five times"; "tap your head two times."

Developmental Considerations
■ Younger children's center of balance changes as they grow, making walking and running even more challenging. They need many chances to fall down and pick themselves up again.
■ As older children hone gross-motor skills, they still struggle to combine tasks such as running and kicking a ball. But they're eager to take on new challenges that aren't too difficult, such as tossing and catching a beanbag, riding a tricycle, or skipping rope.

VISUAL/SPATIAL PERCEPTION

Often an adult and a child can look at the same two objects and "see" them quite differently. An adult's perception is influenced by years of experiences with numerical and logical concepts. A child is just developing the ability to perceive logical relationships among objects. Working with blocks, puzzles, pegboards, and pattern blocks, and moving through small, low spaces and wide open spaces, all help children refine their visual/spatial abilities.

Ways to Assist
■ Use visually descriptive words that relate objects to others, such as "the tallest flower," "the biggest bucket," or "the smallest ball."
■ Encourage children to try puzzles that are at the appropriate level for their visual/spatial abilities. Be sure to have a variety on hand.
■ Offer materials that allow children to create their own visual patterns and shapes.

Developmental Considerations
■ Younger children usually use trial and error when doing puzzles or engaging in other visual/spatial tasks. They may try every piece until one fits.
■ Older children begin to use visual relationships to work through everyday problems, such as studying several blocks to find the right shape or size for the car they're constructing. While children's visual/spatial skills are still fairly undeveloped, the more they're used, the more they're refined.

WITH MATH

COGNITIVE DEVELOPMENT

MATH PROBLEM-SOLVING SKILLS

Problem solving involves applying math in workable ways. And problems to solve using math concepts occur all day long. For example, when four children figure out how to share two apples, that's problem solving. Help develop children's problem-solving skills by encouraging them to brainstorm and test their ideas.

Ways to Assist
■ Create problem-solving situations out of common experiences. If the milk pitcher is empty after pouring several glasses, ask children how much more milk they think it will take to fill the other glasses. Encourage groups to solve problems together as they arise.
■ Don't discourage solutions that seem silly or illogical. If Ryan thinks that the way to find out which of two jars holds more is by weighing the empty jars on a balance scale, help him test his idea to see what conclusions he reaches.

Developmental Considerations
■ Twos and threes are only beginning to predict cause-and-effect relationships. If asked, "What would happen if ... ?" they may say anything. Most can handle only one-step problems based on their own concrete experiences.
■ Fours and fives are starting to solve problems with more logic. They begin to hold mental images (tied to concrete experiences) long enough to visualize what could happen next.

"TALKING MATH"

Each time children put their math thinking into words to share with others, they further their understanding of math concepts and the purpose of language. When Sharmayne tells you how she figured out how many children are taller than she is, she may confirm her own reasoning or uncover a mistake in her logic. These discoveries are a wonderful, natural way to learn math.

Ways to Assist
■ Model language as you solve math problems. "If two children sit at this table and two sit at that one, we only have room for four children. But if I put three chairs at each table, we have room for all six of you."
■ Be patient as children struggle to put thoughts into words. They may need to demonstrate with objects as they explain their math thinking.
■ Plan small-group math activities. This will encourage children to discuss math ideas with peers as well as adults.
■ Use literature to encourage children to verbalize math concepts. As they search the picture for the smallest bunny or the four bluebirds, they can talk through their discoveries.

Developmental Considerations
■ Twos and threes learn language at a rapid pace. Modeling words will help them "talk math," too.
■ Fours and fives tend to be quite verbal, but talking about math concepts that are new and undeveloped in their minds creates a special challenge. Follow the child's lead and let him or her decide when to talk math.

LOGIC & REASONING SKILLS

All mathematics is based on logical reasoning. While most children don't fully develop adult reasoning until adolescence or later, the process begins much earlier. An environment that integrates math learning into everyday routines offers young children much-needed opportunities to try out their emerging reasoning skills.

Ways to Assist
■ Invite children to explain how they get their answers to math questions. If Nora says there is more clay when the same amount is shaped like a cylinder than like a ball, ask how she knows.
■ Model your own reasoning. "If I put three containers of paint at the easel, I need a brush in each one. That's one, two, three brushes."

Developmental Considerations
■ Twos and threes usually can't give logical explanations. But you can model logical reasoning: "This tower has more blocks than that one, so it must be taller."
■ Fours' and fives' attempts at reasoning make more sense, even if they're not totally logical. Four-year-old Paula says there's more water in the tall, skinny glass than in the short, wide one because, "It looks like it."
■ Children's reasoning goes through shifts that accompany mental growth. Correcting a child's logic, even if he or she memorizes the "correct" answers, will not change his way of reasoning until he reaches the next developmental milestone.

SETTING UP
FOR MATH LEARNING

In a room that's set up with math learning in mind, it's hard to tell where the "math area" is, because math learning is occurring almost everywhere you look!

Take a peek in the block area and you see Kristin and Carla carefully estimating what size plank they'll need for their "two-story" structure. Move on to the dramatic-play area and you find Enrique and Hung Sun selecting clothes to fit dolls of different sizes. In the cooking area, Darrell, Tanya, José, and Halley are helping to measure and chop ingredients for apple muffins.

Finally you see Nicole and Charlie counting and sorting seeds, then graphing them on a chart. They're working in the center called the "math-manipulatives area," but clearly, it's far from the only place where math connections are made.

Of course, this kind of everyday math exploration doesn't just happen.

You help it occur. The materials you provide, questions you ask, and learning goals you have for children help provide the setting for math explorations and learning.

IF MATH SHOULD BE INTEGRATED, WHY A "MATH AREA" AT ALL?

Setting up for math does involve planning for math activities throughout the room — and outside, too. At the same time, children need to know where they can always find the pattern blocks; they need to see a shelf filled with puzzles they can do. To organize math learning in your environment, and to interest children in doing activities like sorting, classifying, counting, and patterning on their own, you need a place where math manipulatives are arranged attractively and with children's independent use in mind.

The importance of math manipulatives cannot be overstated. Hands-on, concrete materials provide tactile and visual opportunities for seeing mathematical relationships. These materials help children develop important understandings related to math concepts and offer concrete representations of abstract math ideas. They provide the means for problem solving and for thinking about mathematics. By working with concrete materials, children are able to reflect on these experiences — to visualize the patterns they create; to count four blocks and grasp that "4" means four objects; to see that a square has straight sides and a circle does not.

Your math-manipulatives area will form the "hub" of much of the math learning in your environment. Skills and concepts developed there will be tested again in other areas of the room. And just as likely, a new discovery made elsewhere will be repeated, in a different way, with the manipulatives in the math area.

The six pages that follow will help you get started in organizing your room for explorations in math. You'll find ideas, as well as a detailed diagram, for setting up a math-manipulatives area or for rearranging an existing one. And you'll find tips on materials to offer and activities to suggest that will enhance math experiences in other activity areas and on the playground, too.

SETTING-UP BASICS:
FOUR RULES TO REMEMBER

As you begin to survey your room and think about ways to make it more "math-friendly," keep in mind these four rules of thumb. They apply to your math-manipulatives area, as well as to every other area of your environment.

■ *Provide quality materials.* You know that young children are attracted to materials that are appealing to look at and manipulate, or that can be used in a myriad of ways. Math materials should be intrinsically interesting to children — simple scales, fascinating containers to fill up and pour with, small building materials that invite little hands to make things they can describe or compare with those of others, etc. Well-made materials in good condition pique a child's interest.

To ensure safe use, materials should have no sharp edges and not be tempting to eat. Test all math manipulatives in a choke tube before presenting to toddlers, twos, or other young children who are at the stage where they tend to taste test with frequency.

■ *Vary materials to encourage new and different math explorations.* The same containers to fill at the sand table, the same clothes to fit to the same dolls in the housekeeping area, or the same objects to sort in the manipulatives area will bore children in time and discourage them from making new discoveries that can lead to new math understandings. Yet too many materials to choose from tends to overwhelm children, especially younger ones.

To keep your learning environment fresh and interesting, rotate materials available in each area, moving some to storage or trying them in other areas for a while, to see what children do with them. Model enthusiasm whenever you introduce new materials into any activity area, but try not to dictate usage. Let children come up with their own ideas first!

■ *Set up materials to encourage children to explore on their own.* Math learning materials should not demand constant adult supervision. Select materials with an eye toward independent use. Then organize your learning areas so that children can choose materials on their own and return them without assistance. That's not to say your presence is not important when children are exploring with math. It is. But your role should be that of observer, guide, and questioner, to extend their thinking.

■ *Plan for children to learn together.* As children play together and share math explorations, they learn from each

EVERYDAY MATERIALS FOR EVERYDAY MATH

Looking for more ideas for materials to stock in your math-manipulatives area? Although quality commercial products are available for developing and reinforcing math processes, you'll most likely be able to offer children a greater and more interesting assortment of manipulatives if you also consider the multitude of common items you can collect to inspire hands-on explorations.

Here's a starter list of materials to look for, both everyday items and commercial products. Many of the everyday materials are recyclable ones that families might contribute. Send a note home now and then asking for specific items to save for math activities. Be sure to station a large receptacle near your entrance so families know where to deposit their saved materials when they drop off children each day.

EVERYDAY MATERIALS

▼ acorns and seeds
▼ ice cream sticks
▼ plastic jars and lids
▼ plastic bread tags
▼ old marbles

other through observation and discussion. Children filling cups at the sand table, for example, may conclude that, "This cup holds more sand than that cup." They're drawing comparisons of volume, an important math concept.

Encourage this kind of shared play and learning by having enough similar materials, and especially sets of objects such as interlocking blocks or geoboards, so that more than one child can comfortably use the materials at the same time. Children won't always play together when they're using the same materials, but even as they work alongside each other, they'll watch and learn from one another's discoveries.

CREATING A "HUB" FOR HANDS-ON MATH LEARNING

Like any other key center in your room, the math-manipulatives area should be a regular, carefully planned part of your environment. Its design should invite children to help themselves to the materials and spend as much time as they need to explore.

The diagram on pages 26-27 pictures a suggested setup. Naturally, you'll want to adjust this plan to your own physical space and to meet the needs of your group. But it offers some basic guidelines to consider as you create your own blueprint. Here are highlights of what you'll see developed in the illustrated diagram.

■ *Location and arrangement* — This will be a fairly quiet space, though you certainly want children to feel they can talk easily with others and not have to stifle a shout when they make a new discovery. Overall, it's best to place it away from noisy areas like the block or gross-motor area. Use low, open shelves to form the boundaries and to separate this area from others.

■ *Furnishings* — Along with the shelving units, which you'll use for storing materials, you'll also need flat — and preferably spacious — surfaces

for children to work on. Set up one large table or two or three smaller ones, depending on your overall space. While you want to provide places where children can work together, don't crowd the area with tables. If you have a soft, low-pile carpet on the floor, children will be just as happy to work there.

Organize storage on the shelves to promote independent use — and independent cleanup! For example, label deep-sided trays or bins with pictures of the materials inside. Then paste corresponding pictures on the shelves where each tray or bin belongs. You're setting up an orderly center and encouraging the use of matching skills each time children retrieve materials.

■ *Materials* — Now what do you provide? Start with an interesting assortment of puzzles with a range of difficulty levels to accommodate the skill levels within your group. Puzzles for younger children should have finger grips and a limited number of pieces. Puzzles for older children can range from framed puzzles to simple jigsaw types.

Games are another good addition to the manipulatives center. Spinner games that require simple one-to-one correspondence as children move game pieces around the board — spin three and move three, or spin yellow and move to the next yellow square — are appropriate for older preschoolers. Memory games and simple card games are also fine for older preschoolers. Uncomplicated number-cube games provide practice with counting and coordination of playing pieces.

There are also many "recyclable" and simple, often inexpensive materials you can stock that will encourage explorations that develop specific skills and concepts. Here's a starter list:

■ *Patterning and sorting*: Buttons, plastic lids, bread tags, and attribute shapes.
■ *Ordering and seriating*: Paint-sample books, and shoe strings of different lengths.
■ *Counting*: Sets of counters, such as chips, cubes, buttons, and marbles.

Materials for counting should include multiple sets of the same materials, to help children see relationships between groups of objects. For example, when there are plenty of same-sized cubes to manipulate, it's easier for children to see that two cubes stacked one on top of the other makes a shorter tower than four cubes arranged the same way.

■ *Visual/spatial understanding*: Geoboards, parquetry pattern blocks, tangrams, and other materials with interesting shapes.

■ *Measuring*: A covered tub filled with sand (with plenty of containers for filling and emptying), pieces of string of different lengths, strips of paper, and tape measures.

For a helpful summary list of materials to consider for your math-manipulatives center, see the sidebar, "Everyday Materials for Everyday Math."

GUIDING LEARNING IN THE MANIPULATIVES AREA

Whether planned or spontaneous, activities in the math-manipulatives area should provide for informal, rather than formal, learning. And naturally, they should all be hands-on. After all, this is a manipulatives area. It shouldn't be a place where trace-the-number or color-five-bunnies worksheets are found.

As you schedule use, remember that children will need plenty of time to develop ideas and to explore with materials. If they feel rushed, the math connections they make will be weak or haphazard.

As you observe, look for ways to extend children's learning. You might suggest another way to use a material or offer a new one. Posing stimulating questions, commenting on what children are doing, and showing genuine interest in what they're thinking will also encourage them to find their own ways to explore. Their involvement and responses will provide cues for further questions and clues into their thinking.

Plan your math-manipulatives area carefully. It's one of the most important ways you can encourage children's math learning. If you set up a comfortable, inviting place where children can work alone or with others, using materials that are attractive and intriguing, you'll have done more for children's math learning than you can imagine. You'll have created a setting where children want to explore, to think, and to solve problems for themselves.

LEARNING MATH IN ALL THE FUN PLACES

With your math-manipulatives area in order, turn your math eye to the rest of the room. Nearly every area of an early childhood environment is ripe for math explorations. Here you'll find ideas for enhancing math connections in the sand/water, art, block, cooking, and dramatic-play areas, as well as on the playground. And a box on page 28 lists books with math concepts to feature in your library corner. Use these suggestions to help inspire your own ideas of how to enhance math experiences throughout your environment.

■**Sand/Water Center**

The possibilities for learning about size, weight, and volume are endless at the water and sand tables. And children's natural affinity for sand and water means so many opportunities for learning to occur!

Make the most of these elements by providing containers of different shapes and sizes to fill, such as buckets, tubs, cups, and cartons. Containers of the same shape in two or three sizes encourage children to really focus on size differences and to compare the amount each holds.

You'll promote geometry connections, too, when you provide containers that offer early experience with the meaning of solid shapes, such as cubes and spheres. For example, use milk cartons for square containers, and plastic margarine tubs for round ones.

(continued on page 28)

▼ old buttons
▼ shoe strings
▼ number cubes (dice)
▼ poker chips
▼ colored blocks
▼ wooden blocks of all shapes and sizes
▼ clothespins
▼ beads
▼ pegs
▼ keys and locks
▼ nuts and bolts
▼ measuring cups
▼ measuring spoons

COMMERCIALLY AVAILABLE MATERIALS

▼ wooden puzzles
▼ geoboards
▼ pegboards
▼ Cuisenaire rods
▼ pattern blocks
▼ pattern cards
▼ Unifix cubes
▼ tangrams
▼ attribute blocks
▼ Lincoln Logs and Legos
▼ pan balance scales
▼ tape measures
▼ board and card games

As you select materials, consider whether each one promotes children's active involvement.

CONSIDER HEALTH AND SAFETY. Children, after all, will be touching these items, and germs are spread easily by hands. Wash recycled items before giving them to children to play with. Clean all math manipulatives from time to time. Make sure any material a two or young three might swallow stays well out of their reach. Reserve those items for older preschoolers' play.

A SUPER SETUP!

Your math-manipulatives area is an important part of your room. Make it a comfortable, inviting place, where children can work alone or with others to explore math in their own ways.

This diagram offers a suggested setup for the area. Naturally, alter it to fit your own space and needs. The numbers on the diagram highlight important elements you'll want to include, whatever the final blueprint.

1 Use low, open shelves to form the boundaries of the area and to separate it from other play areas. Three shelves work well and provide plenty of storage space for math manipulatives.

2 Offer children a spacious, flat surface and room to work together by pro-

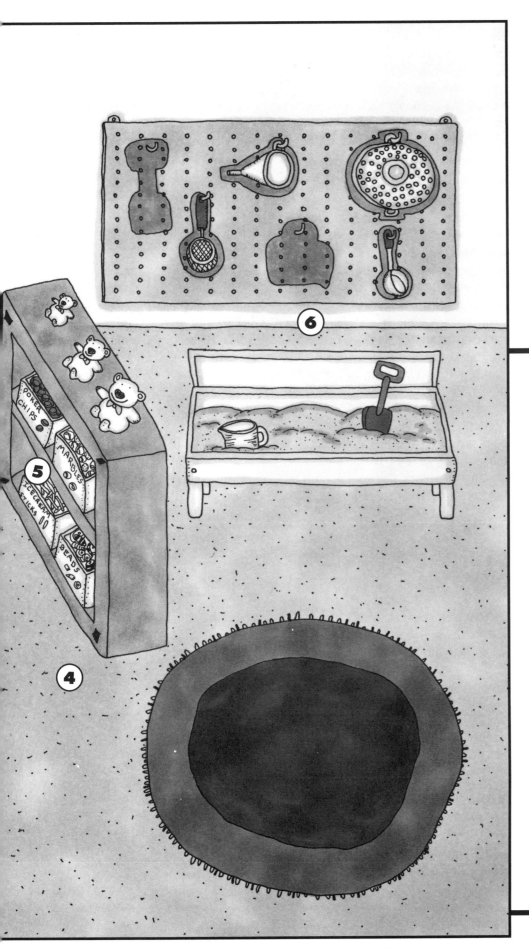

viding a large table and four child-sized chairs.

3 If your space is limited, one or two small round tables also provide places to work together.

4 Allow for plenty of open floor space, too. A low-pile carpet will encourage children to play here.

5 Store materials in bins and trays on the open shelves. A picture of the items inside each bin, and a corresponding picture on the shelf, encourages matching skills and makes cleaning up easier.

6 A nearby sand/water area offers another cleanup matching exercise. Here children hang up containers and utensils by matching an object to an outline of its shape on a pegboard.

7 Add some color and whimsy to your walls. Look for posters of numbers or geometric shapes shown in child-appealing ways.

Make cleanup time a mathematical exercise as well, in this area and in others. Here's a basic idea to adapt: On an empty wall or pegboard next to the area, at children's height, draw an outline of the shape of each material and add a hook to hold it. When it's time to clean up, a child matches object to shape outline, then hangs it on the hook.

■ Block Area

Block play is a very natural way for children to learn about relationships between and among solid shapes. Children need little direction to construct with blocks. Even very young children will stack them into simple towers. A math experience evolves as they discover that two large blocks make a tower the same size as four smaller blocks. Older preschoolers build with an idea in mind, such as a garage for the tractor. As children make decisions about how they'll put the blocks together and which block they need next, they use mathematical problem solving. As they look for blocks of a particular size or shape, they estimate, use geometry, and measure.

To pique children's interest in your block area, offer blocks in different sizes — from small unit blocks to large hollow ones — and of different materials, such as wood, cardboard, and foam rubber. Be sure to provide blocks with interesting geometric shapes, such as cylinders, curves, ramps, and planks. Interlocking blocks will inspire different kinds of structures from those that stack.

Accessory items in the area enhance math learning, too. Wheeled toys, for example, stimulate conversations about which car goes faster.

■ Dramatic Play

Think math as you select materials for your dramatic-play area. Clothes to fit dolls, furniture for miniature houses, different-sized dishes, and pots and pans of many sizes, colors, and shapes all lead to mathematical discoveries.

To encourage use of one-to-one correspondence, every plate should be partnered with a spoon, knife, and fork. Each pan should have a lid to fit. Each shoe should have a mate.

Promote buying and selling scenarios by providing play money and priced

MATH AT STORYTIME?
IT FIGURES!

Counting books, shape books, and books that ask children to classify objects or make comparisons, such as noting objects that are big or little, integrate math into storytime in fun, meaningful ways. Here are a dozen books to consider for your library corner. Many are familiar stories you may already have. You'll also find more books with math themes in the activity plans, pages 38-77.

COUNTING BOOKS

▼ *Anno's Counting Book* by Mitsumasa Anno (Harper & Row)

▼ *Over in the Meadow*, illustrated by David Carter (Scholastic)

▼ *Rooster's Off to See the World* by Eric Carle (Picture Book Studio)

▼ *So Many Cats* by Beatrice Schenk de Regniers (Houghton Mifflin)

SHAPE BOOKS

▼ *Boxes! Boxes!* by Leonard Everett Fisher (Viking)

▼ *Changes, Changes* by Pat Hutchins (Macmillan)

▼ *Circles, Triangles, and Squares* by Tana Hoban (Macmillan)

▼ *Shapes* by Jan Pienkowksi (Harvey House)

BOOKS FOR CLASSIFYING & COMPARING

▼ *Bigger and Smaller* by Robert Froman (Thomas Y. Crowell)

▼ *Crash! Bang! Boom!* by Peter Spier (Doubleday)

▼ *Is It Red? Is It Yellow? Is It Blue?* by Tana Hoban (Greenwillow Books)

▼ *The Very Hungry Caterpillar* by Eric Carle (Putnam)

items. Displaying a simple scale may prompt a pretend mom or dad or doctor to weigh the baby. Jars with lids can encourage matching. An adding machine, shoe-size measurer, and tape measure help stimulate pretend play with numbers.

■ Cooking Area

Cooking is a natural way to learn math skills and concepts. As children measure cups of flour, follow the order of the recipe, and time the finished product in the oven, they're engaging in math. Recipes with lots of easy-to-read diagrams and simple steps help children learn to read math symbols such as fractions. Children also solve problems as they discover that four half-cups is the equivalent of two cups. And they can count — the apples for the applesauce, and the eggs to go into the batter. Older preschoolers may even reason that if two of the four eggs have been added, we must need two more.

Children learn one-to-one correspondence as they make one muffin for each person in the class and put one slice of cheese on each miniature pizza. They begin to gain a concept of temperature as they set the oven to 450 degrees and a concept of time as they eagerly wait the 15 minutes it takes the pizzas to cook.

The key to encouraging math learning in the cooking area is to let children do it themselves, working and problem solving together. Sure, it'll get messy. But that's a sign that children are actively involved, learning math and more!

■ Art Area

As children experiment with art materials, such as paints, paper, and clay, they begin to see relationships that lead to mathematical thinking. As they fill the paper with countless dots of red paint or coat the whole page with dark paint to look like "night," they're discovering visual/spatial relationships. As they put the red paintbrush into the red paint jar, they're matching by color. As they pinch and push clay into forms they call "pancakes" and "donuts," they're recognizing and representing

these foods by shape — a visual/spatial/geometric skill.

Look for ways to build in experiences with math in the art area. Children will be classifying, for example, when they must put the red markers in the red can and the blue markers in the blue can. They'll practice counting and one-to-one correspondence when there's a peg for each smock. And when encouraged to work independently, they quite naturally get meaningful opportunities to solve problems — such as "How can I clean up my own mess?"

■ The Playground and Beyond

Exploring outdoors, on the playground and beyond, offers many math-rich experiences. There are exciting math discoveries to discuss, such as when children splash through a puddle and leave wet bootprints behind, creating interesting patterns on the pavement. Comparing trees to find the biggest one and counting the steps to the top of the slide are other ways children naturally integrate math skills into outdoor play.

You can promote math connections on the playground by drawing large geometric paths — circles, triangles, and squares — for children to follow on foot or while riding a tricycle or other wheeled toy. As children examine everything from interesting seed pods to animal footprints, ask questions to help them classify their discoveries by shape, color, size, or other clues. Encourage children to look for leaves and flower petals that are similar in shape or color.

Neighborhood walks are wonderful opportunities to "think math." As you amble down the street, look for signs of different shapes, numerals on the houses and apartments, and patterns in the sidewalk. And you're sure to find many objects to compare: the height of the trees, the shape of the windows in the buildings, or the weight of two beautiful stones you find along the way.

As you point out these and other relationships to children, they will begin to observe so much around them — math connections, of course, and a whole lot more!

ENGAGING CHILDREN WITH
SPECIAL NEEDS IN MATH

Learning math through play is just as appropriate for a special-needs child as for other children. In fact, it's even more important for these children to experience math in natural ways, so they can learn at their own pace, in a setting that helps them recognize how math is part of everyday life.

There are, of course, differences in how you'll approach math learning with special-needs children. Visually impaired children, for example, who lack the ability to see relationships among objects, will need special help to fully develop many math skills and concepts. Mentally retarded children will need more direct assistance to get the most from math experiences. But your goal will continue to be to build on the play activities that interest each child, using materials that are available to the whole group.

The ideas that follow are general suggestions for engaging children with particular conditions in hands-on math learning. Use these guidelines, along with specific advice from children's family members and therapists, to develop an approach to math learning tailored to each special child.

MENTALLY RETARDED CHILDREN

These children need more time and practice to learn concepts than other children, as well as more opportunities to repeat the same activities over and over. Hands-on math learning affords this to children because they can engage in play that develops math skills — like filling different-sized containers at the water table — again and again.

Tips and techniques for working with a mentally retarded child:

■ Give the child plenty of time to become familiar with the shape, weight, size, and other basic characteristics of play materials.

■ Encourage him or her to play near a child who is using similar math materials, such as those used to sort and classify, to get ideas on how to use and explore with those materials.

■ Let the child play with the same materials over and over, looking for ways to extend the play whenever appropriate. For example, if a child repeatedly places triangular and square blocks randomly in a line, compliment her on the long line. Then demonstrate making another line that arranges the blocks in a pattern of square/triangle, square/triangle. Mentally retarded children often need to be gently pushed to try new learning challenges.

■ As the child engages in different types of play, look for opportunities to "talk math." As you interact, use math words related to shape ("Look at all the squares!"), number ("You put two spoons by each plate."), length ("Here's a longer paint brush."), weight ("Which stone feels heavy?"), etc.

■ Encourage the child to work with a smaller number of materials, so that she doesn't become overwhelmed. For example, if a group of children is comparing three objects by size, she might compare only two.

■ When classifying and comparing objects or creating patterns, be sure the child is working with objects that have obvious differences. It's easier to sort circles and triangles than circles and ovals, for example. The circles and tri-

angles should all be the same size and color, so she'll look only at differences in shape.

■ Encourage the child to repeat any activity that is new to her over again the same day. Frequent practice will help cement a new skill. To keep her attention, use a reinforcer, such as providing a bell she can ring when she finishes ordering a set of objects by size.

■ Ensure success. Show the child which block comes next in the pattern, or count the number of objects in a group together. Work to build the child's confidence so that she'll feel able to progress with less and less assistance from you.

VISUALLY IMPAIRED CHILDREN

While other children depend mainly on sight to learn about number, size, shape, and other math concepts, visually impaired children rely on touch and on descriptions from other children and adults. Offering plenty of math manipulatives is even more imperative with these children, as is encouraging hands-on discoveries and verbal interaction with other classmates.

Tips and techniques for working with a visually impaired child:

■ Give the child time to feel math materials to become familiar with their basic properties. Describe the objects to add to what the child learns through touch:

"These are round buttons. Here is a big button. Here is a small button. Can you find another one that feels small to you?"

■ Suggest math-based activities the child can do with materials: "Hold the blocks together. Which one feels longer?" Since the child cannot watch others for ideas, he or she will rely more on verbal suggestions.

■ Encourage children playing near the visually impaired child to describe what they're doing to help the child imitate their use of math materials. Children can also share discoveries that the visually impaired child can understand through touch. "Matt, you've taken the stones and leaves we gathered on our walk and made a pattern with them — one stone, one leaf, one stone, one leaf. Would you show Adam how to do that, too?"

■ Children with visual disabilities often have trouble understanding relationship concepts, such as *big/little* and *long/short*. Use these words as you talk about what the child is doing, and prompt him to use them, too: "That's a tall bucket you're filling up with sand. Now can you find one that feels shorter to fill?"

■ A child with visual impairments will also have difficulty learning number concepts. Include number words frequently in conversation with the child: "You found two stones. Let's count them together — one, two."

■ Emphasize quantity words — *some*, *few*, *many*, *less*, *greater*, *half* — as you observe the child manipulating objects. Cooking activities offer many opportunities to use these terms. As the child measures, cuts, and pours, use quantity words to describe the results.

HEARING-IMPAIRED CHILDREN

Much of the meaning a child gets from math experiences comes from hearing others use math words and identify math relationships, and in talking through his or her own math thinking aloud. A hearing-impaired child's inability to hear others "talk math" and to verbalize his own discoveries easily can delay the child's development in math. Consequently, you'll want to place a special emphasis on helping hearing-impaired children learn the language of math and talk about experiences that develop math skills and aid in understanding concepts.

Tips and techniques for working with a hearing-impaired child:
■ As the child is engaged in math experiences through play, describe what he is doing, using words that identify math relationships (number, shape, and size words, such as *bigger* and *smaller*), patterns the child is making, or ways he's using math to solve problems. The child will more easily link his own actions with math skills and concepts when he's actively engaged in comparing containers of water, for example, or setting the table in the housekeeping center, rather than if you point these connections out to him later on.
■ Encourage the child to talk about what he is doing, and ask questions that promote the use of math words: "Do you have a whole apple or a half of an apple?" "How many cups will you need for your tea party?"
■ When you're demonstrating a skill, such as how to measure the teddy bear's length with string, involve the child directly. Be sure you have his attention as you explain what to do in simple terms. Then invite the child to

measure a second object. Talk through the process again, describing the steps as he measures.
■ Encourage other children to share their math discoveries with the hearing-impaired peer: "Good job, Raul! You figured out how to arrange the blocks from biggest to smallest! Why don't you tell Stephen how to do it?" Remind them to get the peer's attention by gently touching the child, then to look directly at him and speak a little louder.

CHILDREN WITH PHYSICAL IMPAIRMENTS

Children with physical disabilities may miss math experiences because of their inability to manipulate materials as easily as other children. You may need to adapt equipment and to prompt the child to become involved in activities that develop math skills and concepts.

Tips and techniques for working with a physically impaired child:
■ Work with the child's therapist to determine the best adaptation to make in equipment. Simple adjustments include using heavy tape to secure stable objects to a table, such as mixing bowls for a cooking activity, or attaching a broomstick to a dust pan (in case the child drops small manipulatives on the floor) so he or she can scoop them up.
■ Determine a body position that will give the child good balance and control for manipulative activities. You may need to fashion a seat-belt-like strap to hold the child securely in a chair. Or place a tray across the arms of the child's wheelchair to provide a work surface. If the child cannot sit well or control her hands at the midline level, place her on the floor with her chest over a bolster and arms forward. Invite others to join her on the floor, so that she's part of a group.
■ For sand and water play, provide shovels and other implements such as pitchers and containers in a variety of sizes and handle widths. The child can then choose those that are easiest for her to manipulate. (Be sure the water is

warm, as cool water will stiffen joints and make manipulating objects more difficult.)

■ Provide a magnetic board and magnetic numbers, shapes, and objects that the child can use to make sets and patterns, to order numbers, etc. The child can slide the magnets around on the board with greater control, and they're less likely to pop off onto the floor.

CHILDREN WITH BEHAVIOR DISTURBANCES

These children usually display one of three types of extreme behavior: withdrawal, aggression, or hyperactivity. Each type of behavior creates special problems for the child and requires special guidance from you.

Tips and techniques for working with a withdrawn child:

Generally, withdrawn children learn at a normal rate, but they tend to watch others explore math concepts, rather than manipulate objects themselves. They'll need lots of reassurance to take part actively.

■ Invite the child to join others in an activity, such as sorting objects, but don't force him or her to participate. When she's watched for a while, sit nearby and demonstrate a similar activity. Gently describe what you're doing to help guide the child in what she might do. "I'm putting the big pegs in this box and the little ones in that box."

■ Once the child begins to take part in the activity, step away. If she withdraws again after you leave, don't rush back to her. Give her time to adjust to your absence. As needed, step in again in another situation to continue to help ease her into fully participating in math experiences.

Tips and techniques for working with an aggressive child:

Aggressive children also generally learn at a normal rate, but have trouble concentrating on a task without bothering others. Their often disordered behavior detracts from learning and caus-

es them to miss concepts or connections that might be apparent to others.

■ An aggressive child often worries that he or she won't get his fair share. Defuse this concern by giving the child and others playing with him specific materials to use. In a cooking activity, for example, give each child a utensil. Explain how you'll take turns, repeating the plan to the special child: "When we need your spoon to stir the applesauce, it'll be your turn to help."

■ Observe as the child plays with others. If you see signs of aggressive behavior, step in before it gets out of hand. Talk to the child about the behavior and about other ways to solve problems. "Marty doesn't like it when you grab his spoon. What's another way to get it without upsetting him?"

Tips and techniques for working with a hyperactive child:

Hyperactive behavior often interferes greatly with learning because a child has difficulty sitting still, concentrating on a task, and listening to others. Children who exhibit hyperactive behavior also tend to get restless when an activity is challenging, and may give up. They need lots of adult direction to remain calm and concentrate.

■ Don't expect the child to stay with one activity for long. Steer him or her toward short and very interesting activities. For example, at the water table, you might suggest that she pour the big bucket of water on the boat, to watch it sink. Describe what the child is doing to keep her attention on the task and to emphasize the math connections. Once she gets restless, suggest another activity, to prevent her from disrupting others.

■ Children who behave in hyperactive ways also typically experience periods when they are less excitable and more in control. Wait for these times to introduce activities that require some concentration, such as completing a puzzle or counting sets of objects.

Merle Karnes, Ed.D., is a professor of special education at the University of Illinois at Urbana-Champaign.

TALKING WITH FAMILIES
ABOUT YOUNG CHILDREN & MATH

Depending on their own comfort with math, adults may see it as a subject that children must master — the earlier the better — or as one to be avoided for as long as possible! As you talk with families about math learning, keep the following in mind.

COMMUNICATE YOUR PHILOSOPHY OF "DISCOVERY MATH"

The most important message to convey to families is that young children learn math naturally — in play situations that allow them to discover math concepts and test their own math thinking and skills, without fear of failure or concern with "right" answers. Here are suggestions to help families understand and appreciate the value of this child-directed approach.

■ *Seeing is believing.* Whenever schedules allow, encourage family members to stop by to watch children play. Try to observe with each adult, pointing out examples of children engaged in math learning — Juanita and Amy comparing their block towers to decide which is taller; Terrel using one-to-one correspondence as he gives each toy animal at the table a plate and cup.

■ *Put it in writing.* Use materials such as the "Learning and Growing With Math" chart on pages 18-21 to help convey the value of hands-on math learning and demonstrate how math supports every area of a child's development. Copy it to send home, or include a section at a time in your program newsletter. Also, share individual children's math milestones in notes home. When Marsha discovers that the tall, thin jar and the short, wide jar both hold about the same amount of sand, that's a major math development her family should know about! Keep a stack of "happy-gram" notes on hand for recording such proud news.

SUPPORT MATH LEARNING AT HOME

You know that young children go through stages of illogical thinking, such as counting their fingers and getting a different number each time, or basing comparisons of more or less on size so that a nickel is more than a dime, or a set of two elephants is more than ten mice. Most families will need help in learning to expect this kind of thinking. They'll also need your guidance in learning how best to respond to maintain a child's positive view of himself or herself as a capable thinker. (After all, two elephants are much bigger than ten mice!)

The reproducible letter that follows offers a good start in helping families understand how to support their child's math learning at home. Sharing the information on ages and stages in math learning, pages 7 and 8, can also help families better understand what to expect from their child at various ages and developmental levels.

As you communicate with families about children's math experiences, remember that ideas of what is appropriate math learning may have changed greatly since parents were in school. We've come a long way in recognizing that doing math is the best way to learn math, and that making mistakes is a natural part of becoming a math thinker and problem solver. Building this understanding now will help families be more supportive of their child's math learning throughout the school years!

MATH IS AN EVERYDAY DISCOVERY!

Dear Family,

You support your child's math learning at home all the time! When you're folding laundry and ask your child to help you match the socks — that's math. Or while baking a cake, you may ask your child to find the big square pan in the cupboard. Recognizing shapes and sizes are important math skills, too.

Discovering math naturally is the best way for young children to learn math skills, and to develop math thinking at their own pace. Your support is so important because your child's self-confidence will help him or her tackle new math concepts now and in the future. These tips can help you continue to make the most of those exciting, everyday discoveries.

"I have four fingers." It's natural for young children to be illogical in their math thinking, such as counting fingers and getting four one time and five the next. But correcting children may make them doubt their abilities, and, fearing failure, they may stop trying at all. So just encourage your child to keep counting!

"Grandma lives a million miles away!" Young children have little concept of distance or time. Those understandings don't develop until primary school years. You support your child most when you confirm his or her basic thinking: "Yes, Grandma lives very far away."

"How do I make a '3'?" It's natural to feel your child is advancing in math learning when he or she can write numbers. However, it's more important for your child to first understand what "3" means — a group of three objects — than to be able to write the numeral. Wait for your child to show interest in writing numbers, then demonstrate ones with special meaning, like those in your phone number.

"Where is a big shelf for a big book?" Think aloud about simple problems your child can help solve: "This book is a problem. It's too big for this shelf. Can you help me find a shelf that's big enough to hold it?" Be supportive of your child's choice, even if it's too small. Just encourage him or her to try another shelf a little bigger!

"One, two, three steps to the door." Continue to make math a part of everyday activities. Count the steps into buildings. Count the cans you put in your grocery cart. Later, as you unpack them at home, compare the cans to see which are smaller, taller, heavier, etc.

Learning math is really very natural. Together, we can be sure it's fun as well!

Teacher

USING THE
ACTIVITY PLANS

As the name implies, each of the 40 activities that follow presents a plan for encouraging children's math learning through natural, everyday experiences. While the first half of *Learning Through Play: Math* provides you with the understanding of why hands-on experiences are the most appropriate ways to develop mathematical thinking in young children, the next 40 pages offer a clear-cut picture of what child-directed math learning looks, sounds, and feels like through a range of suggested explorations.

TAILOR THE PLANS TO MEET YOUR CHILDREN'S NEEDS

As you review the plans for each age — there are 10 each for twos, threes, fours, and fives — think about your own children and your own daily routines. Is there an outdoor plan that might add a new dimension to your own playground play, or one you'd like to adapt to use at the sand or water table? Perhaps you prefer to just file the plans and pull them out, for example, when you notice children taking a special interest in measuring and need ideas to enhance their discoveries.

The activity plans are designed to be flexible — to be used in the way that most enhances math learning for your children. The format is easy to follow. Each plan includes most of these sections:

- **AIM:** The value of the activity is explained through a list of math skills that are enhanced, as well as other skills that are developed.

- **GROUP SIZE:** The suggested group size is the optimum number of children to involve at one time. Naturally, adjust this number as necessary.

- **MATERIALS:** Everything needed to enjoy the experience is listed here. Most materials called for will be basic ones you'll have in your room.

- **IN ADVANCE:** This occasional heading details special materials to collect or prepare, or arrangements to make, before doing the activity.

- **GETTING READY:** Here you'll find ways to introduce the activity theme to one child, a small group,

or the whole group. Handling manipulatives, exploring together, and drawing out children's own prior experiences are all active ways to set the stage for new math discoveries.

- **BEGIN:** Now the math learning truly gets under way. Here you'll find suggestions for introducing materials and for helping children get started. You'll also find guidance on ways to observe and ask questions to extend — not intrude on or direct — children's mathematical thinking.

- **REMEMBER:** These bulleted tips are filled with developmental reminders of ages and stages in math learning. You may also find a safety precaution here or an art tip that relates to the theme.

- **BOOKS:** Each plan features at least three carefully chosen children's books that enhance, extend, or just put a delightful sense of closure on the math explorations children have enjoyed.

SHARE THEM, TOO

You may duplicate each plan for educational use, so don't hesitate to share! Fellow teachers, aides, and volunteers at school, as well as family members at home, can all benefit from the guidance the plans offer in structuring math explorations with children's interests and age levels in mind. What's more, you share with others a philosophy of child-centered, hands-on math learning — that math is child's play!

USING THE ACTIVITY INDEX

The index on pages 78-79 lists each activity plan, along with the developmental areas and skills it enhances. Use the index to:

▼ Determine the full range of skills and concepts covered in the plans.

▼ Highlight specific skills and developmental areas a plan reinforces when talking with family members.

▼ Identify and locate an activity that reinforces a particular math skill or concept.

▼ Identify activities that complement your group's particular interests.

ACTIVITY PLANS

FOR TWOS, THREES, FOURS, AND FIVES

MATH

Twos will enjoy hunting for natural objects to compare size and weight.

BIG AND LITTLE, HEAVY AND LIGHT

Aim: Children will be introduced to simple comparisons involving size and weight.

Group size: Four to six children.

Materials: A large pan balance scale; several buckets or bags; big and little items such as a big doll and little doll, a big block and little block, and a big book and little book; and items that are heavy or light, such as a feather, book, fabric swatch, and block.

GETTING READY

Gather children and show them a few of the different-sized items. Give them time to investigate the objects on their own. Then hold up the two dolls, for example, and say, "Are these dolls the same? Is one bigger? Which one? Which one is smaller?" Repeat with the other pairs of objects.

If children's interest holds, put these items aside and bring out some of the heavy and light objects. Give children time to handle the objects, then say, "Show me an object that feels heavy when you pick it up. Show me an object that feels light."

Now bring out the balance scale and demonstrate how it works. Leave the items and the scale in your manipulatives area, where children can continue to investigate on their own.

BEGIN

Invite children to go on a nature hunt. Give each a bucket or bag and take a walk around a grassy area. As children roam, point out natural items such as leaves and pieces of fallen tree bark. Encourage children to put these items in their buckets.

When everyone has a few objects, sit together to share your finds. First talk about size, and model the use of descriptive words such as "tiny," "small," "large," and "big." Use phrases such as "bigger than," "smaller than," and "the same as" to compare objects. This will be enough for some twos, who will want to move on to other activities.

Other twos may be ready to go a step further to focus on weight. Encourage them to hold items that are obviously heavy — a rock or a large piece of bark — in one hand, and a light object such as a twig in the other. Help children find the words to compare the weights of these objects and how heavy or light they feel. You can also bring out the scale and let children use it to test the nature items.

Remember

▪ Scout the nature-hunt area beforehand for litter, broken glass, and plants or animals to avoid when investigating there.

▪ Supervise twos carefully as they collect items, and remind them not to destroy living things by picking flowers or pulling off branches. You'll also need to be careful that children do not collect items they could choke on, such as small pebbles or other objects that might not pass a choke-tube test.

▪ This activity is just an introduction to the concepts of size and weight. Don't expect twos to understand these concepts, or what it means to weigh something with the balance scale. Exposure over time will develop true understanding.

BOOKS

Share these books about objects that are big and little, heavy and light.

▪ *Barney Is Big* by Nicki Weiss (Puffin Books)

▪ *The Turnip* by Pierr Morgan (Philomel Books)

▪ *When I Was a Baby* by Catherine Anholt (Little, Brown)

Which ball fits into which hole?

MATH

FUN WITH BALLS AND BOXES

Aim: Children will use visual/spatial and problem-solving skills, as well as eye-hand coordination and language skills.

Group size: Two children.

Materials: Balls of various sizes, such as a tennis ball, large rubber ball, sponge ball, and beach ball; boxes of various sizes, such as a shoebox, small cardboard box, and a large cardboard box; a basket; and scissors or a sharp knife (for teacher use only).

In Advance: Cut a different-sized round hole in each of the cardboard boxes. Make sure the largest ball easily fits into at least one of the holes. Place all the balls in the basket.

GETTING READY

Show children the boxes and the hole in each one. For a concrete test of big and little, invite children to see which holes they can fit their fingers, hands, and legs through. Next, bring out the basket of balls. Give children time to play freely with the balls. As they play, comment on the size of each ball. "Wow, Jeremy, you're holding a big beach ball! Lucy, you have the small tennis ball."

BEGIN

Now place the boxes on the floor. Make sure there is plenty of space between them so that children will not get in each other's way. Demonstrate how the medium-sized ball fits through some of the holes. (It should not fit through all of them.)

Invite children to experiment to see which balls they can fit through which holes. As you observe, help each child find words to describe what is happening as he or she matches balls to holes successfully: "That's right, Leah. That big beach ball fits through that big hole."

When children finish playing, ask them to help you clean up by placing all the balls back in the basket and putting the boxes inside one another or stacking them. Comment on the sizes of the balls and boxes as you do this together.

Remember

- Choose an assortment of balls that are clearly different sizes to aid twos in matching balls to holes.
- Twos are easily overwhelmed by too many choices. You may want to start with just two boxes and two balls, and add more as children become comfortable with the activity.
- Twos' language abilities are developing, but they communicate primarily in short phrases. When modeling language for them, speak in complete sentences.

BOOKS
Enjoy these books about size.

- *Big and Little* by Ruth Krauss (Scholastic)

- *Big or Little?* by Kathy Stinson and Robin Baird Lewis (Harper & Row)

- *Is It Larger? Is It Smaller?* by Tana Hoban (Greenwillow Books)

MATH

Move outdoors for matching skills!

OUTDOOR PICTURE MATCH

Aim: Children will use matching and other beginning number skills as they recognize pictures of common objects and match pictures to real items in their environment.

Group size: Three or four children.

Materials: An instant camera, or catalogs and magazines of playground equipment to cut up; oaktag or cardboard; non-toxic white glue; tongue depressors; plastic lids, pie tins, or other shallow containers; and craft sticks or glue brushes.

In Advance: Choose an outdoor area with which children are very familiar, such as the playground. Select magazine pictures or

take large, clear photographs of various objects found in that area, such as the slide, a swing, and a seesaw.

Cut five to seven five-inch by eight-inch pieces of oaktag or lightweight cardboard. Pour glue into the shallow containers and put out brushes or craft sticks for children to use to apply the glue.

GETTING READY

Invite children to help you with an art project. Ask each child to choose a picture to glue to a piece of cardboard. Then give each a tongue depressor to glue to the bottom of each card, to form a handle. As the children are working, ask questions about the pictures: "What do you see in this picture? Have you seen a swing like this before? Do we have a swing on our playground?" Give children plenty of time to share comments or experiences on the playground that the pictures may bring to mind.

BEGIN

Gather children in the area where the pictured objects are located. Place the pictures children helped you prepare on the ground or on a table. (Do not offer more than five to seven pictures at a time or children will be overwhelmed.) Then invite children to help you solve a problem. Explain that you are sure you have seen each of these playground objects before, but you just can't remember where. As children respond with a look or by pointing toward the playground equipment, hand each child a picture card and ask him or her to match it to the actual object. Provide plenty of verbal praise: "Yes, Cindy, that is our swing. Thank you for helping me find it!"

Remember

▪ Plan ahead to insure that all children outdoors are adequately supervised when you are engaged in learning activities like this one. Be sure there are adults who are watching your other twos at play while you work with a small group.

▪ If you use magazine photographs of playground objects, be sure they adequately match your objects and aren't cluttered with extraneous visuals that will confuse children. Large, simple, clear photos work best.

▪ Twos' attention spans will vary. Some children will match one picture and be ready to move on to another activity. Be sure to follow each child's lead.

BOOKS

Share these books to help twos take a closer look at their everyday surroundings.

▪ *Look Around* by Leonard Everett Fisher (Viking Kestrel)

▪ *The Playground* by Harold Roth (Grosset & Dunlap)

▪ *Take Another Look* by Tana Hoban (Greenwillow Books)

MATH

Your twos will want to open and close these "presents" again and again.

CAN YOU TOP THIS?

Aim: Twos will develop visual/spatial, matching, and comparison skills, as well as practice eye-hand coordination.
Group size: One or two children.
Materials: Three different-sized boxes with lids; gift wrap or stickers, markers, and crayons; and various objects from around the room that children select.
In Advance: Put the boxes on a table and remove the lids. You may want to wrap the boxes to look like presents (wrapping box and lid separately). Or put out stickers, markers, and crayons and invite children to decorate the boxes. Be sure that the top and bottom of each box are wrapped or decorated similarly, as a visual clue. (If children are doing the decorating, put out one box at a time and change the color of the markers or the type of stickers so the boxes will look different from one another.)

GETTING READY

Gather one or two children together and place one box, with its top on, in front of them. Give children time to hold the box, shake it, open it, and look inside. Repeat with the other boxes.

BEGIN

Now place the bottoms of all three boxes in front of the children. (Keep the three lids out of sight.) Pull out one lid at a time and offer it to a child. Ask the child if he or she would like to try to find the bottom that "belongs" to the top. Let the child experiment until she gets the lid to fit one of the boxes. You may need to offer a few verbal hints: "Sharon, that lid looks bigger than that box. Can you try it on the big blue box with the puppy-dog sticker on it?" Make sure each child has ample time to experiment with finding matches for each box bottom and top.

What Fits Inside?

To extend the fun, encourage children to experiment to see what objects will fit inside the boxes. Choose one box and ask, "What do you think will fit in this box? Let's see what we find." Encourage children to search the room for objects they think will fit. Give them plenty of time to test their objects in the box. Repeat with the other boxes, for as long as children's interest holds.

Remember

When practicing matching skills with twos:
- Keep the choices simple and fairly obvious.
- Show children a proper match before you ask them to make a match on their own.
- Provide verbal hints, but refrain from making the match for the child.

BOOKS

Here are peekaboo books to enjoy with your twos.	■ *My Presents* by Rod Campbell (Aladdin Books/Macmillan)	■ *Peekaboo* by Mitsumasa Anno (Philomel Books)	■ *Peekaboo Animals* by Bobbi Katz (Random House)

MATH

Color matching is challenging but fun for twos!

EGG-CITING POMPON MATCH

Aim: Children will practice one-to-one correspondence and matching skills, as well as eye-hand coordination and fine-motor skills.

Group size: Individuals, or three or four children.

Materials: An empty egg carton; twelve 1 1/2 inch pompons in three or four colors; markers in the same colors; a large, plastic self-sealing bag (pierced with holes for safety); and a pair of dull-edged plastic tongs.

In Advance: Color the inside of each section of the egg carton to match the color of one pompon: If you have four each of blue, red, and yellow pompons, you should have four sections each of blue, red, and yellow. Put the pompons in the self-sealing bag.

GETTING READY

Add the pompons and egg carton to your math-manipulatives center. Observe how children use the materials on their own. When you notice children placing a pompon in each section or making color matches, reinforce the concept of one-to-one correspondence with the following activity.

BEGIN

Place each pompon in a matching egg-carton section. Close the carton and put it on a table or in a small group area on a rug. Then invite one child or a small group to join you, and help him or her carefully open the carton. One at a time, point to the pompons and say, "Look, one yellow pompon in one yellow hole. One red pompon in one red hole," etc. Encourage children to take turns removing one pompon at a time, placing it on the floor or table in front of them.

Next, invite a child to pick up one pompon and place it in any one hole. Younger twos may need several tries, while older twos may go a step further, putting one pompon in each hole and matching colors as well. Model descriptive language as you observe children's efforts: "Morgan, I see you put the blue pompon into the blue hole!"

A Manipulative Challenge: Add Tongs!

As children become more proficient with one-to-one correspondence and color matching, introduce a new challenge. Provide a pair of plastic tongs for children to use to pick up the pompons and place them in the carton. Be sure to show children how to use the tongs. Give them plenty of time to practice — and praise for trying: "Ellie is using the tongs to pick up one pompon and put it

into one hole! You matched the colors, too! Good job!"

Remember
- Let each child progress at his own pace, mastering each level before moving on to the next.
- To encourage greater success among younger twos, simplify the activity by using only one or two colors.
- Provide twos with plenty of time to experiment with these materials. They may discover new ways to use them, such as by turning the carton over and placing the pompons in the underside sections.
- For variety, set out containers in the same colors as the pompons and invite twos to sort pompons by color at cleanup time.

BOOKS
Share these books about numbers and colors.

- *How Many Kisses Good Night* by Jean Monrad (Random House)
- *The Little Red House* by Norma Jean Sawicki (Lothrop, Lee & Shepard)
- *The Wildlife 1-2-3* by Jan Thornhill (Simon & Schuster)

MATH

Here's a way to "round out" your day!

ROUND AND ROUND

Aim: Children will use visual/spatial and observation skills to recognize round objects and shapes.

Group size: Up to six children.

Materials: Round objects to supplement those already found in the room, such as balls, vehicles with large wheels, a round clock, and a round rug; a large bag containing large round buttons, plastic lids, small balls, plastic rings, and paper or plastic plates; poster board; a cardboard box; markers; tape; glue; cotton balls; and scissors or a knife (for teacher use only).

In Advance: Test all small round objects you have collected in a choke tube. Discard any that a child could swallow. Place the rest in the bag.

Next, create a "Round Rosie" character by cutting a sheet of

poster board into a circle, the bigger the better. With markers, draw large round eyes, a round nose, and round pink cheeks. Cut a round mouth large enough to fit your hand through, and glue on cotton balls for hair. Tape the face onto a large cardboard box so it stands up. Cut a hole in the box where the mouth is.

Finally, survey your room to be sure you have plenty of round objects in it for children to spot.

GETTING READY

Take the bag of round objects and the face you've made to the round rug. Invite several children to meet a new friend. Point out Round Rosie's round eyes, nose, and mouth. Give children plenty of time to look at and touch the face.

BEGIN

Now invite children to look at the other round objects you have gathered. Help them take turns removing an object from the bag. Encourage them to try to identify each object, and model using the word "round" to describe each one. Go slowly. Let twos manipulate the objects and feel their round shapes. Repeat the question, "Is this round? Yes! This is round, too."

Observe to see if any children notice Rosie's open mouth. Some may insert the round objects through the hole on their own. Or you may need to tell children that Rosie is hungry, but that she only eats round objects. Ask children to find some round objects to feed Rosie. Give them plenty of time to put all the round items into Rosie's mouth.

What's Round in Our Room?

Invite interested children to look around the room with you to find more things that are round. You may need to get them started by pointing to a round plate in the housekeeping corner and saying, "Look, this plate is round!" This can become an ongoing activity.

Remember

▪ "Round" is the first shape-related concept children recognize, normally around age two. At this age, a child's scribbling also changes from a side-to-side motion to a circular one.

▪ This is just an introduction. Don't expect children to fully understand the meaning of "round." Concentrate on having fun. With exposure over time, children will learn this and other shapes.

BOOKS

| Share these books about different shapes. | ▪ *Circles, Triangles, and Squares* by Tana Hoban (Macmillan) | ▪ *Little Peeper's Busy Days* by Tiny DeVries (Modern Publishing) | ▪ *Wheels on the Bus* by Raffi (Crown) |

MATH

Three is definitely not a crowd with this flannel-board activity.

SMALL, MEDIUM, LARGE

Aim: Children will practice one-to-one correspondence, as well as classifying, comparing, and ordering objects by size.

Group size: One to three children.

Materials: Paper, pencil, permanent black marker, felt, and a flannel board or an 18-inch by 24-inch piece of cardboard covered in black felt.

In Advance: Make the flannel-board items. Draw a small, medium, and large stick figure on paper to use as patterns. The small figure should be about three to four inches high; the medium figure about five-and-a-half to six-and-a-half inches high; and the large figure about seven to eight inches high. Cut out the figures; then, using a permanent marker, outline the patterns on light-colored felt or flannel. Add details such as eyes, a nose, and a mouth; then cut out the felt people. Cut out a small, medium, and large spoon, bowl, and chair from flannel. Make a felt table by cutting a horizontal line about two inches thick and 12 inches long, with a leg at each end about six inches high.

GETTING READY

Sit on the floor in a carpeted area. Place the felt board in front of you and keep the felt pieces in your lap. Invite a few children to join you on the rug. Share the felt figures with children and give them plenty of time to hold them, feel their soft texture, and observe the different shapes and sizes.

BEGIN

When children have had time to handle the pieces, explain that you are going to use the figures to tell a story about three hungry people. Say, "There was one small person ... " (place the small felt person on the board) " ... and one medium person ... " (place the medium person on the board) " ... and one large person." (Place on the board.) "They were very hungry. Then they found some bowls of food." (Place the bowls on the board, verbally labeling each one as "small," "medium," and "large.") Go through the same procedure in placing the spoons and chairs on the board. Then say, "I am going to put the large person in the large chair with the large bowl of soup and give her a large spoon to eat with." Do the same with the other felt persons.

Remove the bowls from the board, then ask one child to give each hungry person a bowl of soup. Observe whether the child matches sizes of bowls with sizes of figures, but don't correct the child if he or she gives a big bowl to the smallest person. Reinforce one-to-one correspondence by emphasizing one bowl for one per-

son. Later, place the flannel pieces and the flannel board in your math-manipulatives center, where children can play with them again on their own.

Remember

- Always sit on the floor at children's level.
- Touching is knowing for twos. Children will gain greater understanding of size comparisons by handling items like the flannel cutouts.
- Twos will find it an exciting change to put felt people on their own bodies. (Pieces should stay on knit or brushed-cotton shirts.) Let them pick the bowl, spoon, and chair which fits their person's size.

BOOKS

Use these books to continue the focus on size.	▪ *Big and Little* by J.P. Miller (Random House)	▪ *How Big Is Baby?* illustrated by Eloise Wilkin (Western)	▪ *Is It Larger? Is It Smaller?* by Tana Hoban (Greenwillow Books)

MATH

As twos empty and fill containers, they experiment with space and volume.

EMPTYING AND FILLING

Aim: Children will develop visual/spatial and measuring skills, while using observation and fine-motor skills.

Group size: One or two children.

Materials: Containers for emptying and filling: old purse, shopping bag, plastic containers, baskets, etc.; a large appliance box; and items to fill containers, such as small toys, balls, plastic-foam squiggles, large buttons, sand, and water.

GETTING READY

Put out a collection of objects to fill and things to fill them with. Twos shouldn't need much prompting to use these items, but if they seem to need an invitation to get started, you might ask, "What can we do with these things?"

BEGIN

Observe as children test the objects to see which and how many will fit inside the different containers. Comparing what the different containers will hold will be easier if you start with similar types, such as three baskets in different sizes. Then encourage children to experiment to see which objects will fit inside the different baskets. Comment on the discoveries you see children make: "Jermaine, you put five big blocks in that big basket!" Prompt with new questions to help children try different combinations: "I wonder how many plastic squiggles will fit in that tiny basket?" or "I wonder if that teddy bear will fit in this small basket?"

Think Big

For a real filling and emptying adventure, offer a very large container, such as an appliance box. Children will enjoy stuffing everything from pillows to toys inside. Of course, the best part is when the box is emptied again and you can exclaim, "Wow, look how many things we put inside this box!"

The Natural Fillers: Sand and Water

This activity naturally extends into sand and water play. Provide a few different sizes of containers for children to experiment with. Comment as you observe children at play: "Dana is using the tiny cup to fill this big plastic jug. It takes many cups of water to fill your jug, doesn't it?"

Remember

▪ As twos empty and fill containers, they are constructing their own knowledge of size, shape, space, and even volume. They can't express these ideas in words, of course, but they are finding out what fits inside a container and what doesn't, or how much something can hold. Such experiences build foundations for future math and science learning.

▪ Too many choices will be confusing to twos. Limit the number of materials available at one time, then change items to maintain twos' interest.

BOOKS

Share these books about filling and emptying — and playing!

▪ *Diggety Dig!* by Harriet Ziefert (Viking)

▪ *Kate's Box* by Kay Chorao (E.P. Dutton)

▪ *Playing* by Helen Oxenbury (Simon & Schuster)

MATH

Make blocks out of boxes, then sort them, too!

SORTING WITH "BLOCK" BOXES

Aim: Children will experiment with classifying and sorting using blocks of various sizes and colors.

Group size: Three or four children.

Materials: Three each of a jewelry-sized, shoe-sized, and grocery-sized box; red, blue, and yellow tempera paint; paint containers; newspaper; large paintbrushes; smocks; and wooden blocks.

GETTING READY

Gather children in a circle. Share some wooden blocks and let

children play freely with them for a while. Then observe aloud, "Look at the different ways you play with blocks. Margaret and Ryan are building a tower, then letting it fall down. It looks like Lei is making a road."

Now introduce one of each size box. Point out the similar shape of the blocks and boxes. Then say, "Let's make our own special blocks using these boxes. First we'll paint them. Then we can play with them."

BEGIN

Before you paint, help twos crumple up newspaper and stuff it into the large grocery boxes. Then use strong tape to close each of the boxes, small and large.

As children paint, talk about the color of the paint they are using and the size of the different boxes: "Whitney, I see you are using red to paint the box. Is it a big box or a little box?"

Playing and Sorting

After the boxes have been painted and have dried, invite children to play freely with them. As they play, talk about the colors and sizes of the boxes.

Later, help children sort the boxes, first by color, then by size. To sort by color, place all the boxes together. Next, place one box of each color in a separate area on the floor. Together, name the color of each of the three boxes. Then point to a box and ask a child to put that box in the pile with another box of the same color: "Alex, this is a red box. Can you show me another red box like this one? Can you put it next to this red box?" Ask other children to find other colors until all the boxes have been sorted.

Repeat the same process using the words "big," "medium," and "little" for sorting the boxes by size.

Leave the boxes in the block area for children to sort and play with in their own ways.

Remember

■ To emphasize each color, you may want to allow three days to paint, using one color each day.

■ As children play with the boxes, point out any patterns you see children spontaneously creating with the different colors or sizes. For example, "Bea, you have a red box and a yellow box and a red box. Can you find another yellow box to go next?" Don't expect children to understand the concept of a pattern. Just aim to increase their awareness by pointing out repeating colors or sizes.

BOOKS

Share these books when you finish sorting.

■ *Boxes! Boxes!* by Leonard Everett Fisher (Viking)

■ *Colors to Talk About* by Leo Lionni (Pantheon)

■ *My Very First Book of Colors* by Eric Carle (Thomas Y. Crowell)

MATH

Invite twos to bring problem-solving skills to playtime.

WHAT CAN WE DO?

Aim: Children will practice one-to-one correspondence and use reasoning skills to solve everyday problems.
Group size: Four children.
Materials: A well-stocked dramatic-play area, with a doll, blanket, bowl, spoon, and other baby-care items for each child, as well as one each for you.

GETTING READY

Set out the bowls, spoons, blankets, and other items in your dramatic-play area. Invite children to join you. Give a doll to each child and let each play with the doll in his or her own way for a while. Reinforce one-to-one correspondence by pointing out that each baby doll has one blanket, spoon, bib, etc.

BEGIN

Introduce a problem situation by asking, "My baby is hungry. Is yours? What can we use to feed them?" Encourage children to look for things to eat with. As necessary, point to the items you set out and ask, "Can we use any of these?"

Continue to pose other problem situations for children to solve, such as, "My baby is sleepy. Is yours? What can we do? What do we need to put our babies to sleep?" Encourage language development by holding up a blanket or pillow and asking, "What's this? Can we use it to give our babies a nap?"

As children collect items for their babies, some may take all the blankets or all the spoons, and conflicts will arise. Help children learn to recognize and solve these real-life problems, too. You might say, "Justin has two spoons for his baby and Trisha doesn't have any for hers. What can we do?" Encourage children to think about the problem and help them verbalize ideas for solving it. Then step back and observe as children handle new situations that occur. If necessary, intervene to ask, "What can we do?"

Remember

Helping children recognize and solve conflicts is an important step toward developing self-control. To assist twos:
▪ Be sure there are enough items so every child can feel ownership. Twos must learn this concept before they can understand sharing.
▪ Have a toy or other object ready to give to a child who may end up without a disputed item.
▪ Help children express their feelings of anger and disappointment in acceptable ways.
▪ Keep in mind that twos' concept of fairness is different from

adults: A child holding a doll may feel completely equal to a child with two blankets and three bowls.
▪ As they play, some twos may emerge as verbal and commanding, while others may be quiet and follow the lead. Still others may engage in parallel play, alone yet near the group. All of these styles are normal for growing twos.

BOOKS

| Share these books about problems and feelings. | ▪ *I Didn't Want to Be Nice* by Jones Orlando (Bradbury Press) | ▪ *I Was So Mad* by Mercer Mayer (Western) | ▪ *MINE!* by Linda Hayward (Random House) |

MATH

Threes can make graphs when they use real objects!

LET'S MAKE A GRAPH

Aim: Children will observe, compare, classify, and count objects in this simple introduction to graphing.

Group size: Three or four children.

Materials: Large sheets of butcher paper or a roll of mural paper; markers; a ruler; clear adhesive paper; and a set of objects to graph, such as toy vehicles (cars, planes, and boats) or blocks of different sizes, shapes, and colors.

In Advance: Make a large sheet of graph paper from butcher or mural paper. Use a ruler to divide the paper into columns, then divide the columns into boxes. Be sure the boxes are big enough to hold the largest items you plan to graph. You'll need as many boxes as you have items in a set. Cover the graph with clear adhesive paper so it will hold up to repeated use.

GETTING READY

Set out a group of objects to sort and graph. Give children time to examine the objects, then talk about them. Discuss how they are the same and how they're different. For example, if you're looking at a collection of toy vehicles, hold up a small blue car. Ask children to find another object in the collection that is like the car in some way. For example, if a child tells you a truck is like a car because it has wheels, ask the other children to find all the items in the collection that they think belong with the car and truck and put them together in one pile. Then select another item without wheels, like a boat. Look at it together and ask children to find others like it. Classify together until all of the objects are sorted into piles.

BEGIN

Now ask, "Which pile do you think has the most items in it?" Give children time to estimate and make predictions. Then bring out the graph paper and help children take one item from the first pile and place it in a box in the first column. Continue placing all the objects from the same pile in the boxes in the first column until you've exhausted the first pile. Then move to the second pile and use the second column. After you've placed all of those objects, say, "Let's look at all the columns of toys. Which one do you think has more than the others?" Because the objects are in columns that are side by side, most children will be able to say which column has more. You might count the items together, to confirm children's answers.

Remember

▪ This will be a popular activity with threes, so let them make graphs whenever they wish. This kind of concrete experience with graphing and counting, repeated over and over, enhances children's understanding of these math concepts.

BOOKS

Share these books that focus on numbers and counting.

▪ *Clementine's Winter Wardrobe* by Kate Spohn (Orchard)

▪ *My Silly Book of Counting* by Susan Amerikaner (Silver Press)

▪ *26 Letters and 99 Cents* by Tana Hoban (William Morrow & Co.)

MATH

Now create three-dimensional graphs together!

GRAPHING WITH PICTURE CUBES

Aim: Children will use creative and fine-motor skills as they develop graphing and counting skills.

Group size: Four or five children.

Materials: Large half-gallon milk or juice cartons (one per child); old newspaper or newsprint; sheets of oaktag the size of the open ends of the cartons; heavy tape; tempera paint thickened with liquid detergent; paintbrushes; clear tape or adhesive paper; and squares of white paper cut smaller than the bottom of the cartons.

In Advance: Ask family members and staff to save half-gallon milk or juice cartons for this activity. Rinse each one, then cut off the top to form a cube. Stuff each lightly with newspaper (ask children to help with this step), then tape oaktag over the open end, to form an enclosed cube.

GETTING READY

Give each child a carton "cube" to decorate. Encourage children to use the thickened tempera to paint the entire outside of the carton, including the bottom. (The bottom will become the front of the graphing cube.) Next, give children a square of white paper on which to draw their own picture. Write each child's name on the completed picture.

When the cubes are dry, help children attach their pictures to the bottom of the cubes using clear tape or clear adhesive paper.

BEGIN

Use the cubes as a concrete, three-dimensional way to familiarize children with the idea of a graph as a way of comparing amounts. Since the cubes can be manipulated by children, they will feel very involved in the graph making.

Graphing the number of boys and girls in your group is one way to introduce the cubes. Make a simple drawing to represent a boy and one to represent a girl. Place the drawings on a table or the floor. Then ask children to place their cubes in a row or in a tower in the appropriate category, with their pictures facing up. When all cubes are placed, talk about the graph. Ask, "What do you notice about the two columns we made? Which do we have the most of today, boys or girls? Let's count and see."

Encourage children to suggest other things you can graph with the picture cubes, such as eye color, hair color, favorite colors, favorite foods, and so on.

Remember

▪ Be sure to have a drawing, photograph, or an actual item to label

each category when children are making the graphing towers or columns. Without this, children may not realize which category they are choosing.

▪ You can also use the cubes for predicting and estimating activities. For example, when using a ramp and balls, have children place their cubes at the spot where they think the ball will stop rolling. Or ask children to predict tomorrow's weather by placing their cubes in the column featuring a specific weather picture, such as a bright sun or raindrops.

BOOKS

Share these books that deal with different math concepts.

▪ *Boxes! Boxes!* by Leonard E. Fisher (Viking Kestral)

▪ *How Far Is Far?* by Alfred Tresselt (Parents Magazine Press)

▪ *Is It Larger? Is It Smaller?* by Tana Hoban (Greenwillow Books)

MATH

Math and matching go hand in hand!

MATCHING CONTAINERS AND LIDS

Aim: Children will practice visual/spatial skills, matching, and one-to-one correspondence, as well as fine-motor skills.

Group size: Two or three children.

Materials: Plastic containers with matching lids in a variety of sizes, a large box or basket, and small plastic or wooden objects.

In Advance: Ask family members and staff to help you collect household containers with lids, such as margarine tubs, takeout-food containers, and old plastic bowls. Invite threes to help wash the containers and lids (a job they'll love!), dry them, and place them in a large box or basket.

GETTING READY

Place the box or basket with the containers and lids in your math-manipulatives center for children to play with on their own. Observe to see how different children use these items. Some will immediately start to match lids to containers, while others may try to fit the containers inside one another. As appropriate, emphasize one-to-one correspondence by pointing out that there is one container top for each container bottom.

As you observe, watch for a child who becomes frustrated or repetitive in his or her play. She might be ready to interact with you in the following ways.

BEGIN

Sit with the child and watch for a while, then comment on what you see the child doing. You might say, "I see you are having trouble matching that round top to that square container. Is there another container you might try?" or "That square container is very large. What size container do you think will fit inside it?" Use comparative phrases such as "the same as," "bigger than," and "smaller than" as you describe the different containers. As children hear these terms, they will begin to incorporate them into their own vocabularies.

Do It Another Way!

Another day, put out small objects for children to place in the containers. Observe as they fill the containers, shake them to make noise, or just fill and empty, fill and empty. Watch for children who may be ready to count and compare how many objects they can put inside two containers of different sizes.

Remember

▪ This activity is a meaningful, concrete experience that grows out of children's interests and lets each child work at her own level. Store the materials where children can use them in their own ways anytime.

BOOKS

Share these stories about household objects at circle time.

▪ *At Home* by Colin McNaughton (Philomel Books)

▪ *The Cupboard* by John Burningham (Harper & Row)

▪ *My Kitchen* by Harlow Rockwell (Greenwillow Books)

MATH

Everyone is bigger and smaller than something. Have fun finding out what.

BIGGER THAN A BREAD BOX

Aim: Children will use observation, visual/spatial, and measuring skills as they compare their bodies to items that are bigger or smaller than they are.

Group size: Three or four children.

Materials: Chart paper and a black marker, and everyday inside and outside items.

GETTING READY

Young children are very interested in size and often compare their own size to objects around them. When you see this happening naturally, introduce this activity. Gather a small group of interested children and ask, "Are you bigger or smaller than a library book? Our pet hamster? A big tower of blocks?" If they are comparing their size to something smaller, such as a pet hamster, you might say, "Are you bigger than anything else? Let's walk around the room and find some things you are bigger than." Then stroll around the room and encourage children to point to objects they think are smaller than themselves.

BEGIN

Return to your group area. Write "I am bigger than ... " at the top of a sheet of chart paper, and read the words to children. Then ask them to name objects they identified as being smaller than themselves. As they name items, let them retrieve the item or go over to it to check their judgment. Ask, "Are you really bigger than that teddy bear, or is the teddy bear bigger than you?" Encourage children to lie down, sit, or stand next to an object, to confirm that they are bigger. As children are satisfied that they are bigger than a given item, record the item name on the chart. Later, some children may want to draw or cut out pictures of each item, to illustrate the list.

What's Bigger Than Me?

Another time, look together for objects that are larger than the children. This is a good activity to do outdoors, where children are smaller than many things, such as trees and playground equipment. It's also easy for children to stand next to these items to make their visual comparisons. Back inside, make another chart-paper list of objects under the heading "I am smaller than ... " Or, if it's not a windy day, bring the chart paper outside and make the list as you go along.

Remember

- Threes are naturally interested in the size of things. Rather than stress who is the biggest, this activity can help someone who is feeling "too small." After all, everyone is bigger than something!
- Children may enjoy finding things that are bigger or smaller than you or another adult.
- Use your findings to talk about similarities and differences in people's sizes. Reaffirm that every size is the right size.

BOOKS
Share these books about size.

- *A Flower Grows* by Ken Robbins (Dial Books)
- *The Tomato* by Barrie Watts (Silver Burdett)
- *The Turnip* by Pierr Morgan (Philomel Books)

MATH

Create simple patterns with this no-cook recipe.

FRUIT-KEBAB PATTERNS

Aim: Children will use fine-motor skills as they practice observation, matching, and patterning skills.

Group size: Four or five children.

Ingredients: Fruit (fresh or canned in light syrup or water) such as grapes, bananas, pineapple chunks, mandarin orange sections, and sliced pears or peaches.

Materials: Bamboo skewers (at least two per child), dull plastic knives, paper plates, napkins, and a bowl for each type of fruit; and large five- by seven-inch index cards, markers, and clear adhesive paper.

In Advance: Prepare the recipe cards. Draw a simple fruit pattern on each index card. For example, picture an orange slice, followed by a grape, another orange slice, and another grape. Make several cards using different fruit combinations. Keep the patterns simple — four to six pieces of fruit per card. Then cover each card with clear adhesive paper for durability.

GETTING READY

Ask children to help you prepare the fruit. First have everyone wash their hands. Then set children to work washing fruit, taking grapes off the stem, peeling and slicing bananas, cutting fruit into chunks, and placing each type of fruit in a separate bowl. Encourage children to talk about the different fruits they see. Ask, "Who has eaten any of these fruits before? Who can tell me the name of a fruit you see? Which kind of fruit do you like the best?" Let children taste as they work. Which fruit do they like the most? Which do they like the least?

BEGIN

Now introduce the recipe cards. Together, talk about how family members and cooks in restaurants use recipes to prepare food. Say, "These are picture recipe cards that show how to make fruit kebabs. Let's follow one." Help children put fruit on their skewers as pictured on the card. Set those kebabs on a plate.

Put all the cards out and ask children to choose one. Help them follow the pattern and place the appropriate fruit on a stick. Then place the finished kebabs aside to enjoy at snacktime.

Let's Eat!

At snacktime, ask one child to pass out the fruit kebabs. Encourage children to describe the different fruit patterns on their sticks. You might show the recipe cards and see if children can match their kebabs to the cards. Then invite everyone to eat!

Remember

▪ Vary the activity another time by making vegetable kebabs with carrots, celery, and green and red pepper.

▪ Some threes will only want to eat the fruit kebab they make. You may want to schedule this activity just before snacktime, so children can create their fruit pattern, then eat it immediately.

▪ Don't worry if children don't match the patterns on the recipe cards perfectly. With practice, they'll improve in matching and recognizing patterns.

▪ Look together for other simple patterns in your room, such as two repeating colors in a floor pattern.

BOOKS

Whet your appetite with these books about food.

▪ *Blueberries for Sal* by Robert McCloskey (Viking)

▪ *Fresh Cider and Pie* by Franz Brandenberg (Macmillan)

▪ *The Very Hungry Caterpillar* by Eric Carle (Putnam Publishing Group)

MATH

Have fun sorting objects from outside!

SORTING AND CLASSIFYING OUTDOORS

Aim: Children will sort and classify an assortment of natural items.

Group size: Whole group for collecting; four or five children at a time for sorting.

Materials: Small paper bags, a marker, and paper plates.

GETTING READY

Explain that when they go outdoors today, you would like children to collect some objects that interest them. Set rules for choosing objects. Help children understand that they should not pull up plants or break off branches. Talk about the kinds of things children might collect, such as unusual stones, odd-shaped pieces of bark, fallen leaves, and seed pods.

Write each child's name on a paper bag, and hand out the bags.

BEGIN

Now head outdoors to the playground or a park. Let children take their time. Threes love the "treasure hunt" atmosphere. As they discover items, talk about their finds. Encourage them to name and describe the different objects.

Let's Sort What We Found

If you have a small group, you may want to sit together outside in a sunny spot to do a sorting activity. Or have children bring their treasures inside, to sort in small groups during the day.

First set up categories for sorting. For example, ask children to sort all the big things on one paper plate and all the small things on another. Place sample objects on the plates as a guide. As children sort, comment on their choices. Ask them to share why they are putting something on a certain plate. Then put all the objects in one big pile and sort again using other categories, such as by color or texture.

Sorting Green Things

There is more than one color of green in our world, and this activity will help children see different shades. Start with a "green" walk. Ask threes to collect only objects that are green.

After the walk, ask children to sort the "greens" onto paper plates. Start with two categories of great contrast — dark green and light green. From there, try to create smaller and smaller piles of objects with more subtle shades of light and dark green. Count the number of objects in each pile.

Remember

▪ Children may have different ideas about why an object belongs in a certain pile than an adult would. Always ask children for their reasoning, and be accepting of it, even if it seems flawed. With time, their logic will improve. The idea of sorting is what is important now.

▪ Ahead of time, scout out areas where children will look for objects to be sure there are no harmful plants or animals to avoid. Plan for adequate supervision by limiting the number of children looking for objects at one time, or have plenty of adult aides.

BOOKS

Share these books to inspire your nature hunters.

▪ *A Day in the Woods* by Ronald M. Fisher (National Geographic Society)

▪ *At the Park* by Colin McNaughton (Philomel Books)

▪ *A Tree Is Nice* by Janice Udry (Harper & Row)

MATH

Here's a sorting activity that children can really sink their teeth into!

CRISPY CRACKER MATCH

Aim: Children will use observation, matching, sorting, classifying, visual/spatial, and fine-motor skills.

Group size: Three or four children, or the whole group.

Ingredients: Round, square, triangular, and rectangular snack crackers, soft cream cheese or butter, and raisins.

Materials: Dull plastic knives, a large bowl, paper plates, napkins, and child-made place mats. For place mats you will need: white construction paper; pre-cut circles, squares, rectangles, and triangles (enough for each child to have a few of each); a marker; paste or glue; and clear adhesive paper.

In Advance: Make the special snack place mats. Give each child a piece of white construction paper divided into four equal sections. Put the pre-cut circles and the glue or paste in the center of the table. Invite children to pick out and glue a few circles in one section. Repeat with the other shapes until children have pasted a different set of shapes in each section. Write each child's name on the back of his or her place mat, then cover with clear adhesive paper.

GETTING READY

Hand out place mats to a small group of children. Sit on the floor together, with a place mat in front of each child. Point to one of the shapes on a place mat and ask, "Can you find a shape like this one?" Then let children point to or physically find an object in the room that matches that shape. Continue to look for other objects in the room that match other shapes on the place mat for as long as children's interest holds.

BEGIN

Ask children to wash their hands, then gather at the snack table. Put out a large bowl and the crackers, and help children pour the crackers into the bowl. Observe to see if children notice the different shapes. Ask, "Who can find two crackers that are the same? Who can find two crackers that are different?"

Help children wipe their place mats and set them on the snack table. Invite one child to hand out paper plates and another to pass the crackers. Each child should put a few crackers onto his paper plate.

Now sit down for snack. Ask children to look at their place mats and review the shapes together. Then say, "Take a cracker and see which shape it matches on your place mat." Invite children to make matches until they exhaust their cracker supply. Comment on what you observe. "Carmen has four round crackers covering

her circles on the place mat. Jorge has made three matches. I see two triangles and a square."

When children have made all their matches, set out the cream cheese or butter, raisins, and plastic knives. Invite children to eat their crackers plain or with a topping. You might comment as you see the shape matches disappearing: "Oh, I see Ivan eating a square. Now Beth is eating up all her rectangles!"

Remember

■ Don't worry if children cannot name the different shapes. The activity is meant to give children practice in matching shapes, not in memorizing circle, square, triangle, etc.

BOOKS

| Share some shape books while children snack! | ■ *Edward and the Boxes* by Dorothy Marino (Lippincott) | ■ *Shapes and Things* by Tana Hoban (Macmillan) | ■ *Square Is a Shape* by Sharon Lerner (Lerner) |

MATH

Here's another fun way to practice recognizing shapes — to music!

LET'S PLAY MUSICAL SHAPES

Aim: Children will practice recognizing shapes and play cooperatively, while using gross-motor skills.

Group size: Whole group.

Materials: Masking tape and/or large cutout paper shapes, and instrumental music.

In Advance: In an open area of the room, use masking tape to form very large geometric shapes on the floor (or use large cutout shapes taped securely to the floor). Aim to have at least three each of the basic shapes — circle, square, and triangle.

GETTING READY

Point out the shapes on the floor. Walk around each shape and name it with the help of the children. Next, invite children to identify matching shapes. Ask, "Who can stand on a triangle? Now, who can stand on another triangle?" Repeat for each shape. (Remember that children may not know the shape names and will need clues to know to which shape you are referring.)

BEGIN

Play a warm-up game that helps children get the feeling of the shapes. Put on gentle music, and invite two or three children to walk around the outside of a shape. Start them at the top or at a corner of the shape and have them walk slowly around the edge, moving clockwise. Ask them to try to stay on the tape lines or on the edge of the cutout shape, like a tightrope walker. Then invite

another set of children to outline other shapes. Continue until each child has had a turn.

Let the Game Begin!

Now invite children to play Musical Shapes, a cooperative game that's similar to musical chairs. The object of the game is for everyone to find a particular shape to stand on when the music stops. Nobody is "out" because everyone works together to squeeze onto the shape.

Begin by having the children find places to stand outside of the shapes. Play music and encourage them to move around the shapes any way they wish. Then stop the music and name one of the shapes (for example, "circle"). Tell children to stop moving and find a circle to stand on. Once everyone has at least a toe touching a circle, give children a "round" of applause for cooperating so well. Repeat this process with the other shapes for as long as children's interest holds.

Remember

- Encourage non-competitive games like this one. Everyone gets to enjoy the full activity, and children learn to work together, not against one another.
- This is a game children will want to play often. Repeated exposure to shapes through natural, fun activities like this one will reinforce children's understanding of different shapes, their attributes, and names.

BOOKS

Share these books with threes as they learn more about shapes.

- *Blue Bug's Treasure* by Virginia Poulet (Children's Press)
- *The Little Circle* by Ann Atwood (Charles Scribner's Sons)
- *Things to See: A Child's World of Familiar Objects* by Tom Matthiesen (Platt)

MATH

Same blocks, different building!

LOOK AGAIN!

Aim: Children will observe and compare shapes and sizes and use fine-motor skills as they use the same kinds of blocks to form different structures.

Group size: Two children.

Materials: Two identical sets of unit or table blocks, featuring a variety of shapes and sizes; a shelf, screen, or other visual divider; and a box to hold each set of blocks.

In Advance: Assemble the two sets of blocks in separate boxes. Include about five or six identical blocks in each set.

GETTING READY

Set out the boxes, and give the pair time to examine the different types of blocks in each box. If children don't discover on their own that they have the same blocks in each box, you might say, "Look, I put one small square in each box. Here is a square block. Esther, can you find the same block in the other box?" Help children line up the two sets of blocks so they can see that blocks of the same shape and size are in each box.

BEGIN

Set up a divider and invite each child to play with one box of blocks on either side of the divider. (The children shouldn't be able to see each other building.) Allow plenty of time for both children to build using only the blocks in their boxes. When both are finished, remove the divider so that each child can see what the other has created.

Talk about the block structures and help children compare the two. "Thelma put her big square on the bottom and has the round pillars on top. She put the two triangles on top of the pillars. Esther put the pillars on the floor and used the big square for a roof."

Encourage each child to tell if he or she thinks she still has the same blocks as the other child. If children are unsure, suggest they take their buildings down and line up the blocks, one-to-one, to show that the blocks are still the same.

Remember

▪ This activity can be puzzling for some threes. Children may insist that the blocks are no longer the same when they are arranged differently. Keep the activity fun, but play this and similar games often. Through repeated exposure, children will better understand the concepts at work and develop flexible thinking.

BOOKS

Use these books to enhance the experience.

▪ *Becca Backward, Becca Frontward* by Bruce McMillan (Lothrop, Lee & Shepard)

▪ *Fun With Shapes* by Ron and Atie van de Meer (Putnam Publishing Group)

▪ *Opposites* by Rosalinda Kightley (Little, Brown)

MATH

Old boxes and lids help threes practice math skills!

IF THE SHOE FITS — PUT IT IN!

Aim: Children will practice comparing, estimating, matching by size, problem solving, and decision making as they match an item to a box, then find its lid.

Group size: Three or four children.

Materials: Many boxes of assorted sizes with matching lids, such as a long, flat tie box, a shoebox, a ring box, a rectangular game box, a deep round hat box, and a square wallet box; and items that fit into the boxes, such as a tie, shoes, ring, game board, hat, and wallet.

In Advance: Bring the boxes and lids to group time. Gather children together and show them one box at a time. You might say, "Here is a deep, round box. What do you think can fit in here?" Give children time to guess and talk about their answers together.

Children might like to search the room for items they think will fit in the box. Invite them to try out their estimations, then together make a verbal list of things that fit into the box. You might say, "We found that our drum, red ball, and teddy bear fit into this deep round box." (Remember to ask children to help put away the objects they found.)

BEGIN

Arrange the tie, shoes, ring, game board, hat, and wallet on the floor where children can see them easily. Place the boxes in a row nearby. Now, encourage children to look at all the objects and all the boxes. Invite one child to try to fit an item into a box. Accept any match where the item fits, even if you feel it is not the most appropriate match — shoes in the hat box, for example, or the tie in the game-board box. Next, invite another child to make another match. As the activity progresses, children may find that they need to move previously placed items to make room for others. When everyone is satisfied that all the objects are in the best box, take out the lids. Invite more children to fit the lids onto the boxes.

Now Let's Guess What's Inside!

Another time, start with items in the boxes and the lids on. Help children guess what's inside.

As an accompaniment, you can also read or tell children a version of "Goldilocks and the Three Bears." Emphasize the relative sizes of the bowls, chairs, and beds — "too big," "too small," and "just right."

Remember

▪ Be sure the boxes and lids are in good condition. Reinforce corners with masking tape, if necessary.

▪ Allow plenty of time for children to make several tries until they find an appropriate box. They may decide to shift items inside the box, or move previously placed items to new boxes. This is great problem-solving and decision-making practice.

▪ Use descriptive language. Help your threes expand their comparison vocabulary with phrases such as "not big enough," "too small," "too long," or "not wide enough."

BOOKS

Share these books about size with your threes.

▪ *The Biggest Bear* by Lynd Ward (Scholastic)

▪ *Everything Has a Shape and Everything Has a Size* by Bernice Kohn (Prentice-Hall)

▪ *Let's Find Out What's Big and Small* by C. Shapp (Franklin Watts)

ACTIVITY PLAN
READY-TO-USE TEACHING IDEAS FOR FOURS

MATH

Help four-year-olds see, hear, and say patterns as they create their own patterning chants.

PATTERNS ARE EVERYWHERE!

Aim: Children will use the mathematical skills of patterning to notice and create patterns with objects, pictures, hand clapping, and words.

Group size: Four or five children.

Materials: Collections of a variety of objects — buttons, bottle caps, small cars, pencils, etc.; and magazine pictures and stickers of animals and objects.

GETTING READY

Patterning is a mathematical concept, but it is verbal and auditory, too. This activity will help children experience patterns with their eyes and ears, and with words. Start talking about patterns by using a few objects to make a simple, repetitive pattern; bottle cap, button, bottle cap, button. Ask children to "read" the pattern they see. Then ask them what comes next in the pattern. Together, say the pattern over a few times as a chant.

BEGIN

Once children feel comfortable "reading" and chanting patterns, move on to helping them create their own. Begin with simple patterns like the one above. (These are called "ABA" patterns because each element is repeated once, one after the other.) Invite children to choose two different objects, such as a toy car and a pencil, and arrange them one after the other to form a pattern.

Encourage them to make the pattern as long as they'd like and to chant it with you.

Next, introduce movements to go along with the chanting. Take one of their patterns and help children choose a movement to go with each element in the pattern. For instance, you might clap when you chant "bottle cap" and pat your knees when you chant "button." Now you are creating patterns that everyone can see, hear, and experience.

Look around the room for ABA patterns on the walls, windows, and people's clothes. Chant them together — you might find "blue stripe, yellow stripe, blue stripe, yellow stripe" on Tanya's shirt; or "glass, metal, glass, metal" on the windows. You'll find children's awareness of patterns is heightened by these activities. They may start chanting patterns they make with blocks, manipulatives, and even their snacks.

Remember
- It's not necessary for children to understand the term "ABA," just to have practice with these kinds of patterns.
- Incorporate people with disabilities into your discussions of recognizing patterns. For example, you could ask children, "What if someone couldn't see patterns with his or her eyes? What are some other ways that person could experience patterns?"
- Encourage children to explore more complex patterns.

BOOKS

Enjoy these books and records about patterns.

- *The Dot and the Line* by Norton Juster (Random House)
- *Edward and the Boxes* by Dorothy Marino (Lippincott)
- "Copy Cat" from the record *Kidding Around with Greg and Steve* (Youngheart Records)

MATH

Here's a simple movement activity children will ask to do again and again.

MOVING PATTERNS

Aim: Children will practice patterning while they use gross-motor, listening, and direction-following skills.

Group size: Small groups or your whole group.

Materials: A drum; rhythm sticks; large construction-paper shapes; several items to make patterns, such as two spoons and two forks, or two crayons and two pieces of paper; and masking tape.

GETTING READY

Talk about patterns. Put out a few items in an obvious pattern: crayon/paper/crayon/paper, or spoon/fork/spoon/fork. You might say, "These items are in a pattern. See how they're in the same order, over and over again?"

Then, using a rhythmic voice, point to each item in order and name it. Invite children to clap along and name the items. Tell children, "We can see the pattern with our eyes, feel the pattern with our hands, and hear the pattern with our ears." Allow plenty of time for children to experience different patterns using their eyes, hands, and ears.

BEGIN

Ask children to join you in a large open area for a movement activity and say, "Can anyone think of a way to make a pattern using your whole body?" Demonstrate a few movement patterns such as step/step/jump, step/step/jump; or hop/hop/step, hop/hop/step. Encourage children to say and clap the pattern as you make the movements. Then invite children to move in the pattern with you. You might use a drum to beat the pattern as everyone moves. Continue as long as children are interested — the longer they move, the more they will feel the pattern.

Next, ask if anyone would like to make up new movements to your pattern. Suggest that everyone sit while one child moves in a pattern to the beat of a drum; beat-beat-pause, beat-beat-pause. Remind the child that to make a pattern he or she must do the same series of movements again and again. Encourage others to help by saying the movements aloud and clapping. For example, the child might turn, clap, then sit while everyone chants, "Turn-clap-sit, turn-clap-sit," as you beat the drum.

Follow the Pattern Road

Another time, form a pattern by taping shapes to the floor. Invite children, one at a time, to follow the pattern as you help them say the name of each shape. For example, your "pattern path" might be circle/square/circle/square. Repeat it as many times as space allows.

Remember:

■ Keep patterns simple at first. Children can make them longer and more complex as they become accustomed to the activity.

BOOKS

Enjoy these music and movement stories together.

■ *Something Special for Me* by Vera Williams (Greenwillow Books)

■ *The Troll Music* by Anita Lobel (Harper & Row)

■ *The Old Banjo* by Dennis Haseley (Macmillan)

MATH

Fours can explore your room and increase their measurement skills at the same time.

LET'S GO ON A MEASURING TREASURE HUNT

Aim: Children will use measurement, observation, comparison, and recording skills.

Group size: Four or five children.

Materials: Brightly colored yarn; construction or newsprint paper; crayons; markers; tape; and a ruler, yardstick, or tape measure (optional).

In Advance: Cut the yarn into pieces of different lengths. Make sure some of the pieces are the same length as objects around your room.

GETTING READY

Talk about measurement. Show children a ruler, yardstick, or tape measure to demonstrate the usual ways people measure things. Then say, "We don't have to use these tools to measure how long something is. We can use anything to measure, even our hands!" Invite children to take turns measuring nearby objects with their hands. Ask, "How many hands long is the bookcase? The rug? The table?" After children have had time to practice, ask them to try to estimate how many hands they think an object will be before they measure it.

BEGIN

Show the pieces of yarn to the group and ask each child to choose a piece to use on a measuring "treasure hunt." You might say, "Look around the room and find one thing that is the same size as your piece of yarn." Demonstrate by choosing a piece of yarn and inviting children to follow you around the room as you hold your yarn up against different items in the room. Help children see and understand how to measure and how to check if the yarn and the object are the same length.

Now encourage children to take their pieces of yarn around the room to find objects the same length. Enjoy the excitement as children find objects that "match"!

Record It!

Record children's measurement "findings" on long sheets of paper laid sideways. Each time a child takes a measurement, tape his or her piece of yarn across the paper, write her name, and write or draw a picture of the "matching" object. Then encourage the child to pick out a new piece of yarn and look again. Take time to look at the chart together.

Leave sections of yarn in the math-manipulatives center, along with a chart of different objects to measure. This way, children can play the game over and over again!

Remember

■ As an extension, consider asking children to compare lengths of yarn. Then help them arrange the yarn in order of length. This will give them practice in seriation, another math skill.

BOOKS

Increase children's understanding of measurement with these delightful stories.

■ *Inch by Inch* by Leo Lionni (Astor-Honor)

■ *One Step Two* by Charlotte Zolotow (Lothrop, Lee & Shepard)

■ *Big and Little, Up and Down* by Ethel Berkley (Addison-Wesley)

1 2 3 MATH

Help fours practice matching skills and gain a better understanding of where things are in the room!

I KNOW WHERE IT IS!

Aim: Children will practice matching and one-to-one correspondence skills.

Group size: Four children or the whole group.

Materials: The only material you need for this activity is your room!

In Advance: Help children explore your room by taking a short "walk" to a different area each day. Gather in that area and invite children to open cupboards and containers and experiment with the different materials and equipment they find.

GETTING READY

When you are ready to do this activity, encourage children to gather a few (up to five) small items from each area of the room. They might choose crayons, plastic spoons, wooden beads, small plastic building pieces, leaves from your science area, and so on. Help children group the items — all the crayons together, all the beads, etc. Now make a game! Put out three-by-five cards and glue. Invite children to glue one, two, or three of the same items on each card.

BEGIN

Put the cards out where children can see them, and invite everyone to come look. Ask each child if he or she would like to choose a card and talk about the objects on it. Next, ask if anyone has seen the objects on the card anywhere else in the room. Encourage children to take a card with them and walk around the room looking for the items on their card. As children begin to find items easily, suggest that they match the items they find, one-to-one, with the items on the card.

Remember

▪ It's important for fours to have lots of time to explore new surroundings. This is a good beginning-of-the-year activity to help them become familiar with your setting.

▪ Matching and one-to-one correspondence are prerequisites to counting. Young children need practice with concrete experiences like these before any counting has meaning. Remember, too, that young children always need concrete objects to count — rote counting is not a meaningful experience.

BOOKS

Here are books filled with pictures to match and pattern.

▪ *The Button Box* by Margarette S. Reid (E.P. Dutton)

▪ *Ten Little Mice* by Joyce Dunbar (Harcourt Brace Jovanovich)

▪ *When One Cat Woke Up* by Judy Astley (Dial Books)

MATH

Go on a nature hunt with a classifying and sorting twist.

NATURE SORTING

Aim: Children will observe, sort, classify, and graph nature materials that they have collected outdoors.

Group size: Three or four children.

Materials: Paper bags (one per child); nature objects such as leaves, nuts, sticks, and stones; a large sheet of paper for graphing; paper plates; crayons; and tape or glue.

GETTING READY

Before you gather your group together, collect samples of natural objects children might see outside your window. Next, invite everyone to stand at the window, look outside, and talk about the things they see. Gather in a circle and make a list of the objects children have mentioned. Explain that today you are going on a hunt to collect all kinds of nature objects. Talk about the kinds of things children can collect (objects that have fallen to the ground, such as leaves and nuts) and share your samples. Also talk about things they shouldn't collect (objects that are still living, such as leaves on trees or objects that are unsafe).

BEGIN

Give children small paper bags to put their objects in. Bring everyone outside and let the nature search begin. If possible, divide children into groups of three or four, with an adult accompanying each group.

When the collecting is finished, ask children to bring their bags inside. Now it's time to sort and classify. With each group, look at the objects collected. Ask, "How are these objects the same? How are they different?" Invite children to sort their objects into piles or onto different paper plates. Sorting categories might include type of item, shape, size, color, texture, etc. As the children are sorting, help them name the categories they are using.

Make a Graph

Now prepare a large graph with your children using a marker or crayon to divide the paper into vertical columns, one for each type of nature object. Divide these columns into squares. Leave room at the bottom of each column so children can tape or glue the appropriate object to that spot. Demonstrate how to place the object inside each square.

Invite children to use the rest of their nature objects to make a mural. After the mural is completed, use it to inspire a story about the nature hunt.

Remember

■ Check your outdoor area beforehand to be sure it is safe for children. Remind them about safety rules for that area, such as staying on the grass or keeping away from swings when others are on them. Talk with children about things that are not safe to collect, such as broken glass.

■ Foster young children's respect for the environment. Help them understand that items still on trees and bushes are alive, so they should not be collected.

BOOKS

Here are some books about the outdoor changes autumn brings.

■ *Fall Is Here!* by Jane B. Moncure (Children's Press)

■ *Autumn* by Richard Allington and Kathleen Krull (Raintree)

■ *What Happens in the Autumn?* by Suzanne Venino (National Geographic)

MATH

Ready, get set, measure!

AS BIG AS ME!

Aim: Children will practice measuring, observing, comparing, and problem solving.
Group size: Three or four children.
Materials: Yarn, plain white paper, crayons, and scissors.

GETTING READY

Talk about growing. Discuss the different ways children have grown this year and the kinds of growing changes they have noticed. Ask, "How many of you have outgrown some of your clothes? Are you the same size as when you started school this year?" If you took measurements at the beginning of the year, compare them to the children's measurements now. Encourage children to bring in clothes or shoes that are now too small for them and compare them to their present sizes.

BEGIN

Do this activity outside on a sunny day. Ask, "What else grows like you?" Look for signs of growth in plants and trees in your area. (New growth appears as the light area of bright green on the ends of branches and plants.) Use pieces of yarn to measure how much the plants have grown. Ask children to look for the plant that has the most new growth on it.

Help children separate into pairs. Explain that while one child lies down on a clean area, his or her partner measures his length using a long piece of yarn. When one partner has measured out the length he wants, help cut the yarn. Then ask children to trade places.

Next, invite pairs to search the playground together as "measuring teams," measuring other objects using their pieces of yarn. Can they find something on the playground that is bigger than they are? Smaller? What about the same size? At the end of your outdoor time, ask partners to show the group the objects they found that are larger, smaller, and the same size.

How Many "Feet" Long Is the Sandbox?

Offer children plain paper and scissors to make and cut out a tracing of one of their feet. Then ask them to look at various objects in the play area and encourage them to compare: "Using your foot drawing, do you think the sandbox is longer or shorter than the seesaw? How many of your feet tall is the climber?" As children explore and measure using their tracings, help them record the number of "feet" long each item is on a simple picture chart (using tally marks). Later, talk about what you have recorded. Ask, "Which was the longest thing we found? The shortest? The tallest? Did anyone find anything that is the same size as their foot?"

Remember

- Growth is usually a fascinating topic to young children! Consider making this activity part of a theme. You could look together at plant and animal growth, as well as looking further into children's growth.

BOOKS
Use these books as discussion starters about growth and growing up.

- *Bigger and Smaller* by Robert Froman (Thomas Y. Crowell)

- *Blue Sea* by Robert Kalan (Greenwillow Books)

- *The Growing Story* by Robert Krauss (Harper & Row)

MATH

Make your own pan balance scale and use it creatively!

KEEPING YOUR BALANCE

Aim: Children will use the mathematical skills of problem solving, estimation, measurement, and recording.

Group size: Two or four children.

Materials: Two of the following: small sponges, pieces of cloth, small stones, washcloths, paper napkins, and pencils. (These should be about the same size.) To make a pan balance: sharp scissors or a small knife (for teacher's use only), one rigid plastic hanger, two plastic bowls or margarine tubs, and string or yarn.

In Advance: Prepare for this activity by making a pan balance. Use the scissors or knife to cut or punch four small holes along the edge of each of the bowls or tubs. (Make the holes across from each other, like the markings of north, south, east, and west on a map.) Cut eight pieces of string. Tie one string to each hole. Tie the loose ends of the strings so the bowls hang freely from each end of the hanger. To use the pan balance, hang the hook from a string or from a child's hand so the entire scale is suspended in air.

GETTING READY

If possible, go out to a playground and demonstrate balance on a seesaw. Invite children to take part in demonstrations to help them see that when a heavier object or person is placed on one side of the seesaw, the other side goes up. Inside or outside, use your homemade balance to show how the balance goes down on the heavier side and up on the lighter side. Ask, "How will the scale move if I put a heavy rock on this side? What will happen when I take it off?"

BEGIN

Now show children the pairs of items you collected. Ask them to put one of each pair in the bowls of the scale. Ask, "How does the pan balance look? Are the two bowls hanging at about the same level? Is one lower or higher? Do they weigh about the same?"

Next, remove one item from each pair. Put two of the remaining objects on the pan and ask, "How does our pan balance look now? Which object weighs more? How can we make them weigh the same?" Discuss this question, and if children don't suggest it, say, "Can we add another item to one side to make it balance?" Encourage children to find items they think will make the scale balance. Ask, "Which side should we add this item to?" Experiment by adding items one by one.

Encourage everyone to continue experimenting by keeping

your pan balance out near the math-manipulatives area so children can compare the weights of objects — buttons, blocks, etc.

Remember

- The concept of balance can be abstract. Invite children to feel what it is like to be a pan balance by stretching their arms out to their sides and having someone gently pull one hand down or place something heavy in one hand. In this way, children can feel what it is like to be weighted down and tip to one side.
- It's not necessary for the pan to balance exactly, just for children to recognize when it is close. Even when you measure pairs of items, slight differences in size may keep the scale from balancing.

BOOKS

Here are books that talk about other simple machines.

- *Machines* by Anne Rockwell (Macmillan)

- *The True Book of Toys at Work* by John Lewellen (Children's Press)

- *One Way Is Down: A Book About Gravity* by Vera K. Fischer (Little, Brown)

MATH

Four-year-olds are fascinated with cars and trucks. Use their enthusiasm to do a graphing activity.

VEHICLE GRAPHING

Aim: Children will observe, count, and graph neighborhood vehicles.

Group size: Four or five children.

Materials: Large sheets of plain white paper, divided equally into boxes, to create oversized graph paper; magazine pictures of different types of vehicles; crayons; and trays.

GETTING READY

Share photographs and illustrations of a variety of vehicles. Ask, "How do we know something is a vehicle? How are vehicles alike?" Talk about how vehicles have wheels, people can drive them, etc.

BEGIN

During an outdoor activity time, invite a group of children to observe the vehicles that go by. You could say, "I wonder how many vehicles go by our playground? Let's find out!"

Explain that you can find out "how many" by keeping a count or "tally." Choose an observation spot and help children get situated with tally sheets, crayons, and trays to rest their sheets on so they can write. Say, "Every time you see a vehicle pass, make one line on your paper." You many need to demonstrate and help the first few times. Encourage children to continue watching and tallying as long as they are interested.

Make a Graph!

When children are finished tallying, make a graph together to record how many vehicles each child saw. Invite children to write their names or draw symbols of themselves at the bottom of the oversized graph paper. Next, ask children to color the same number of boxes as the number of vehicles they observed. Later, "read" your graph together. You might ask, "Who saw the most vehicles? Who saw the least? Did anyone see the same amount?" Be sure to emphasize that the object is not to see the most vehicles, but to get a chance to tally and graph. You might ask, "Why do you think some children saw more vehicles than others?" (Perhaps children were looking in different directions, or some tallied a longer time than others.)

If children are interested, consider repeating this activity with a twist — each child chooses only one vehicle to tally, such as a truck, or bicycle, or convertible. Use the graph you create to see how many of each kind of vehicle passed your setting.

Remember

▪ This activity may take children in the vicinity of traffic. Be careful to do this only if children are behind a fence, and remind everyone about safety rules before going outside.

▪ Children may become frustrated if there are too many or too few vehicles to tally. You can adapt this activity to your area by tallying and graphing other things that pass by, such as animals or people.

▪ Because it uses symbols instead of concrete objects for graphing, this is a good activity to do after children have had some experience with graphs.

BOOKS

| These books illustrate different types of vehicles. | ▪ *ABC of Cars and Trucks* by Anne Alexander (Doubleday) | ▪ *Big Red Bus* by Ethel and Leonard Kessler (Doubleday) | ▪ *Have You Seen Roads?* by Joanne Oppenheim (Addison-Wesley) |

MATH

Big, bigger, biggest! With this activity, your fours will have hands-on experience.

HOW BIG IS BIGGEST?

Aim: Children will use the math skills of comparison, seriation, and problem-solving, along with observation, language, and group-interaction skills.

Group size: Four or five children.

Materials: One object, such as a small ball, block, apple, or orange; a table for display; experience-chart paper; markers; and a bag or pillowcase filled with objects, each just a little bigger than another.

GETTING READY

Talk about the concept of "big." Invite children to brainstorm a list of all the things they think are big. Record their responses, then review the list together. Ask, "Are all these things the same size? Which ones are bigger than others? Is 'big' just one size?" Then ask, "Which one of these things do you think is the biggest of all?"

BEGIN

Gather a few children to do a big-bigger-biggest activity. Show them the ball (or other object) that you have brought in and then place it on the left edge of the table. (This helps children practice left-to-right progression.) Ask, "Can you find something in this bag that is a little bigger than the ball I put on the table?" Ask a child to reach in the bag, choose an object, and place it on the table next to the ball. Together, compare the size and decide whether or not it is just a little bigger. Next, ask another child to take a turn and look for something just a little bigger than the second object and place it next to the others for comparison. Continue until all the objects in the bag are out and you have created a seriated line of objects across the table.

Look around the room together for the things that are just a little bigger still. Eventually your line may have to go off the table and continue on the floor or onto another table. By the end of the game the biggest thing in line may be a child, or even you!

Another time, start with a medium-sized object on the left edge of the table, and look for something just a little smaller. Continue from left to right, until children find something teeny-tiny for the end — perhaps even drawing a little dot for the smallest thing!

Remember

▪ Emphasize the comparative vocabulary words "big," "bigger," and "biggest."

▪ Help children see that as the line gets longer, things that were considered bigger or even biggest are no longer so. Do not expect them to fully grasp this concept. The point of the activity is to experience it, see it, and use the words.

▪ Set up seriation activities children are able to do themselves, such as arranging graduated sizes of crayons, buttons, or paper footprints.

BOOKS

Share books about size.

▪ *Big and Little* by Joe Kaufman (Golden Books)

▪ *Bigger and Smaller* by Robert Froman (Thomas Y. Crowell)

▪ *Blue Sea* by Robert Kalan (Greenwillow Books)

MATH

What can you do with raisins and water? Make estimations about volume!

HOW MUCH IS THERE?

Aim: Children will use sand and water to observe, estimate, experiment, and evaluate volume.

Group size: Three or four children.

Materials: Plastic containers of various sizes, a tub to hold water, water, measuring cups, chart paper, crayons or markers, and a jar filled with raisins.

In Advance: Prepare a chart by drawing pictures of the containers you are using at the top of chart paper. Underneath each picture, make two columns, one for children's estimations and the other for results. Write children's names down the left side of the chart and draw lines from their names across the paper.

GETTING READY

Talk about making estimations. Explain that when you estimate, you are making a guess based on the things you see. Each time you make an estimation and test it out, you get more information. Help children understand that it's not important to guess the right answer; the important thing is to practice making estimations.

BEGIN

You can practice estimations with the age-old game of guessing how many items are in a jar. Record children's ideas on chart paper, then open the jar and count the number of items. Allow time for children to tell whether their guesses are higher or lower than the actual number. Celebrate the game by eating some of the contents from the jar, then ask, "Now is there more or less in the jar than before? How many do you think are in the jar now?"

Try It With Water!

Show children the collection of plastic containers, and ask them to pick out the ones they think need the most cups and least cups of water to be completely full. Next, take turns estimating how many cups of water will fill each container. Help children use tally marks, dots, or numerals to record their estimations in the appropriate column of the chart. To test the estimations, help children make a tally mark or dot on the paper each time another level cup of water is added to the container. Compare the estimated amount with the actual measurement. Ask, "How close was your estimation? Was it higher or lower than the real number of cups?" Encourage children to try different containers.

Remember

▪ Encourage children to use containers of a variety of shapes and sizes. This will help them as they begin to construct their own theories on volume.

▪ Use language that emphasizes comparing estimations and outcomes — "more than," "less than," "the same as" — rather than calling predictions right or wrong.

▪ When you fill the guessing-game jar, only put in the amount of raisins that your group can comfortably count. More than that may confuse some children.

BOOKS

| Here are books to share about sand and water. | ▪ *The Quicksand Book* by Tomie dePaola (Holiday House) | ▪ *Sand Cake* by Frank Asch (Crown) | ▪ *The Sun, the Wind, and the Rain* by Lisa Peters (Henry Holt) |

MATH

Your fives will begin to see how big they really are with fun, hands-on measurement activities.

"ME" MEASURING

Aim: Children will make observations and estimations and use comparative language and thinking skills as they use their bodies as a unit of measure.

Group size: Four or five children.

Materials: Construction paper; adding-machine tape or ribbon; markers and crayons; yarn; and experience-chart paper.

GETTING READY

Take off your shoe and trace your foot on a piece of paper. Cut out your tracing and show children your "foot picture." Explain that you are going to use the picture to measure things in the setting. Ask children to estimate which items in the room they think are about the same size as your foot. Let each child use the cutout to test his or her guesses. Next, find things that are bigger or smaller than the foot, or ask, "What can you find that is about two of my feet long?"

BEGIN

Help children (and ask them to help one another) each trace a hand and foot on a sheet of construction paper, then cut out the parts. Compare hands and feet. Which are longer? Wider? Are they bigger or smaller than yours?

Estimate together. What items in the room do children think are about the same size as your foot? Record their ideas on an experience chart. Next, encourage children to check out their guesses using their cutouts. Try other estimations. What objects are about two or three hands long? Can they build something that is about two hands long?

I Am This Tall

Use adding-machine tape or ribbon to measure children's heights. Encourage them to take their "Me Strips" around the room to find objects that are the same size, bigger, or smaller. Save the strips for end-of-the-year comparisons.

Remember

• Young children may feel badly if their estimations are interpreted as "wrong." Remember, the purpose of this activity is to practice skills — not guess a "right" answer!

• Avoid recording children's names when you record their estimations, as this can lead to talk about whose guess was "right."

• Some children may feel uncomfortable about taking off their shoes. Just let them trace around their shoe instead.

BOOKS

Here are some good books about children and growing.	■ *Peter's Chair* by Ezra Jack Keats (Harper & Row)	■ *Where I Begin* by Sarah Abbott (Coward)	■ *The Growing Story* by Ruth Krauss (Harper & Row)

MATH

Enjoy this hands-on experience with area and volume together.

FILL 'ER UP!

Aim: Children will use problem-solving, creative-thinking, and fine-motor skills as they make discoveries about volume and area.
Group size: Four or five children at a time.
Materials: Unit blocks, small table blocks, masking tape, construction paper, scissors, experience-chart paper, markers, large cardboard cutouts of basic shapes, and a variety of different-sized and -shaped boxes.

GETTING READY

At circle time, talk about the cardboard shapes and help children name them. Then invite children to match objects in the room to those shapes. Together, use your memories to brainstorm objects children may have seen other places that are the same shapes.

BEGIN

Tape a few cardboard shapes to the floor and encourage children to cover them with different-shaped unit blocks. Tell children the idea of this game is to cover as much of the shape as possible without overlapping any blocks, leaving empty spaces, or letting any blocks hang over the edge. You could say, "It's like doing a puzzle with blocks as your puzzle pieces." When all the shapes are full, talk about differences between the shapes and the blocks that are needed to fill them. Ask, "Which shape needs the most blocks to fill it? Let's count. Which shapes are the most difficult to fill this way? Why?" Give children time to think about their answers. Then put out a smaller set of table blocks and ask, "Do you think we will need more or less of these smaller blocks to fill the shapes?" Suggest that children test their predictions by playing the same game.

Experimenting With Volume

Another time, put out the unit blocks, table blocks, and several different sizes and shapes of boxes. Invite children to use the bigger unit blocks, and then the smaller table blocks to fill the boxes. Ask thought-provoking questions such as, "Do you think we will need more little blocks or big blocks to fill a box? Which box do you think will hold the most blocks?" Encourage children to carefully pack each box rather than randomly throw the blocks in. Suggest they try to fill each box in a few different ways.

You may want to create an experience chart by listing shape names in a column, and next to them recording the objects children have seen.

Remember
▪ It's important that children try to fill the shapes using at least two types of blocks. This allows them to see that an area can be filled in different ways.
▪ It isn't necessary to use the terms "area" or "volume" with children. It is only important that they experience the concepts.

BOOKS
Share these shape books at storytime.

▪ *Shapes, Shapes, Shapes* by Tana Hoban (Greenwillow Books)

▪ *Square Is a Shape* by Sharon Lerner (Lerner)

▪ *The Little Circle* by Ann Atwood (Charles Scribner's Sons)

MATH

Help your fives explore their room with this beginning-of-the-year sorting game.

CLEANUP-TIME SORTING, PART I

Aim: Children will use sorting, classifying, problem-solving, and thinking skills to organize familiar objects around the room.
Group size: Four or five children.
Materials: Familiar objects such as a toy car, crayon, scissors, dress-up shoe, sieve, shovel, and different manipulative and puzzle pieces; photographs of different play areas of the room (sometimes available in school supply catalogs); and cafeteria trays, construction paper, paper plates, etc., to hold objects.

GETTING READY

Talk with children about the toys and materials found in the different play areas in your room. For example, point to the book corner and ask, "What do you do in this area of the room? What materials can you find here?" Encourage children to notice that certain toys go with particular places. Ask, "Are there any materials that are used in more than one area?" Together, make a list of materials that can be used in several areas. Make tally marks on the list to represent the number of areas next to an item's name.

BEGIN

Next, discuss the objects you have collected. Invite children to name each one and tell something about it — its color, use, where they might find it, etc. Help children decide specific categories and sort the items according to those categories. You can demonstrate by starting to sort objects by color or size and encouraging children to finish. Ask children to sort the objects according to where they are used. If possible, provide pictures or drawings of each area to mark the sorting piles. Encourage everyone to talk about their

thinking as they sort, and to point out similarities and differences they see.

Now invite children to find new items to add to the sorting game. Again, ask them to sort the items in many different ways. End with sorting by play areas.

Putting It All Away

At the end of the game, ask children to put the items away. Here's a song to sing as you do:

> **Cleanup Song**
> (Tune: "The Farmer in the Dell")
> We're putting our toys away.
> We hope it won't take all day.
> We have to get done, so let's have fun.
> We're putting our toys away.
>
> The trucks go in the blocks.
> The trucks go in the blocks.
> We have to get done, so let's have fun.
> The trucks go in the blocks.
> (Change verse to fit the items.)

Remember

▪ Using trays or construction paper as sorting mats helps children focus on the organization of sorting.
▪ Some children might need your help at first to understand how to sort objects.
▪ See "Cleanup-Time Sorting, Part II" for a follow-up.

BOOKS
Try these books at storytime.

▪ *The First Day of School* by Patricia Reif (Western)

▪ *The Awful Mess* by Anne Rockwell (Parents Magazine Press)

▪ *The Big Tidy-Up* by Nora Smaridge (Golden Press)

MATH

Extend cleanup-time sorting into a group graph.

CLEANUP-TIME SORTING, PART II

Aim: Children will use sorting, classifying, problem-solving, and comparison skills to graph familiar objects.

Group size: Four or five children.

Materials: Common preschool materials such as scissors, crayons, paper, pencils, paintbrushes, paint, paste, markers, blocks, puzzle pieces, small interlocking plastic blocks, toy cars, toy dishes, dress-up clothes, paper clips, and measuring cups; spoons, paper plates, and plastic utensils; and cafeteria trays or large sheets of colored construction paper for sorting mats.

In Advance: Make a life-sized graph by dividing a large piece of mural paper into four columns of eight-inch-square boxes. Label each of the four columns a different play area in your setting. Or, to make a permanent, reusable graph, use a light-colored shower curtain liner and mark off columns and boxes with masking tape. The boxes should be big enough to fit the objects children graph.

GETTING READY

Talk with children about the sorting activity you did together. You could say, "Remember when we sorted things in our room, like scissors and puzzle pieces? We put them into special piles." Ask children to recall the ways they sorted objects. Take out the items again and encourage children to group them according to play areas.

BEGIN

Explain that now you are all going to take the sorted objects and arrange them on a graph. Talk about graphing. Have children seen a graph like this before? Point out that categories on the graph correspond to the play areas. (If possible, use copies of the same pictures to label the sorting piles and graph columns.) Then encourage children to place the objects, one per box, in the appropriate columns. Invite them to make comparisons. Which category has the most objects? Which has the least?

If interest is high, encourage children to repeat the activity using other sorting categories.

Remember

▪ Try doing this activity a day or two after the cleanup-time sorting activity. Singing the Cleanup Song again may be a good way to stimulate memories.

▪ Some materials will fit into several categories. Encourage problem-solving skills by asking children, "What ways can you think of to solve this problem?"

▪ Graphing real objects, rather than symbols like colored squares or tally marks, helps young children understand what a graph is and how it works.

▪ Young children need and enjoy lots of practice with graphing. Look for ways to incorporate graphing into other activities in your program.

BOOKS

These books talk about the people and materials in school.	▪ *First Day in School* by Bill Bizen (Doubleday)	▪ *Joshua's Day* by Sandra Surowiecki (Lollipop Power)	▪ *Welcome Roberto* by Mary Serfozo (Follett)

MATH

This creative art activity will encourage children to be more aware of shapes.

CIRCLES AND SQUARES AROUND US

Aim: Children will use geometric shapes to create pictures and sculptures and become more aware of the shapes found in things around them.

Group size: Five or six children.

Materials: Pre-cut geometric shapes made from construction paper and/or origami paper (in at least three sizes and colors); white drawing paper; glue; crayons; masking tape; spare materials with recognizable shapes, such as round plastic lids, small square and rectangular boxes and lids, clean food containers and boxes, and tubes.

GETTING READY

Review shapes with children using the pre-cut construction paper shapes. As you show a shape, invite them to name it. After each shape has been identified, encourage children to find things in the room that are a similar shape. Make an experience chart by dividing the chart into columns, one for each shape (circle, square, triangle, etc.). Record your children's shape findings. Which shape did they find most often?

Make this graph a permanent part of your room. Use pre-cut shapes and place one in the appropriate column for each item found in the room. Make sure shapes are in vertical rows from the bottom to the top of the graph paper.

BEGIN

Show your children a shape. Encourage them to brainstorm things that have that particular shape. For example, a circle is the shape of a clock, a wheel, a doughnut, a swimming pool, a pizza, etc. Repeat this process with other shapes.

Let each child pick one of the pre-cut shapes, and provide him or her with a piece of paper, crayons, and paste. Ask children to choose: They can paste the shapes on their paper and add their own designs, or make their own shape creations without using the pre-cut shapes.

Offer children fresh sheets of paper and an assortment of shapes. Invite them to create scenes, pictures, or designs by pasting the shapes on the paper.

The Shape of "Junk"

Try this shapes-extension activity: Provide children with all types of spare materials to create sculptures. Encourage everyone to examine the materials to find the shapes they want to use. After sculptures are completed, invite children to share about their creations with one another.

Remember

- As with any art activity, be sure to allow children full control over their creations.
- Reinforce the concept of shape by commenting about shapes children choose to use. You could say, "I see you're using lots of triangles in your art."

BOOKS

These shape books may inspire your budding artists.

- *The Little Circle* by Ann Atwood (Charles Scribner's Sons)

- *The Parade of Shapes* by Sylvia Tester (Child's World)

- *Shapes and Things* by Tana Hoban (Macmillan)

MATH

Step outside for a problem-solving shadow activity!

SHADOW PLAY

Aim: Children will use the mathematical skills of measurement, estimation, and problem solving to experiment with their shadows.

Group size: Four to six children.

Materials: Colored chalk; yarn, string, or other objects for measuring; tape; experience-chart paper; mural paper; and markers and crayons.

GETTING READY

Choose a sunny day and go outside together, or put up the window shades and take down the curtains in a particularly sunny room. Then suggest that you go on a shadow hunt. Look for shadows made by trees, buildings, play structures, furniture, and, of course, people. Encourage children to play and experiment with their shadows.

BEGIN

After children have had time to play, gather together to sit and talk. You might say, "I wonder if we could measure our shadows. How do you think we could do that?" If no one suggests it, say, "Maybe we could start by tracing them." Ask children to suggest ways to trace their shadows. What materials will they need? Will they work alone, or will they need partners? Record their ideas on experience-chart paper.

Help children choose partners and gather materials, then encourage them to test out their ideas. They might choose to trace the shadows directly onto hard pavement with chalk. They might want to spread out mural paper on the ground and trace on that with crayons. Or, they might have other ideas. Guide them with open-ended questions as they work. "What can you use to keep the mural paper from rolling up?" "Can you think of something else to use since the chalk doesn't show up on the grass?" When everyone is finished, stand back and admire all the shadows lying about!

Next, ask children for ideas about how to measure their shadows. Again, invite them to suggest ideas, talk about how they will work, and try them out. Use questions to help children to solve any problems they encounter.

Comparing Shadows

Encourage children to compare their shadows. Which is bigger, children or their shadows? Can they find something the same size as their shadow? What ways can they think of to find out?

Remember

▪ Try to be flexible in allowing children to test out their ideas. Consider adopting this rule: An idea is okay to try as long as it is safe, doesn't disturb other people, and doesn't destroy plants or property.

▪ At the same time as you encourage children to think and test, try to keep them from becoming frustrated.

▪ Some fives will be very independent in pursuing ideas; others will prefer to follow someone else's lead.

▪ Open-ended questions have many possible answers, not just "yes" or "no," or one "right" answer. They often start with "What do you think ... ?" or "Can you find a way ... ?"

▪ Children may want to explore other aspects of shadows — when they appear or how they change at different times of day.

BOOKS

Here are shadow books to share.

▪ *Bear Shadow* by Frank Asch (Prentice-Hall)

▪ *Come Out Shadow Wherever You Are!* by Bernice Myers (Scholastic)

▪ *Shadows* by Tara Gomi (Heian International)

MATH

Encourage five-year-olds to use their "beans" while they play these math games!

WHO'S GOT THE BEANS?

Aim: Children will use basic math thinking skills such as estimating, comparing, and counting.
Group size: Three or four children.
Materials: Large, dry kidney beans; a clear jar; paper cups; one die; and a pan balance.

GETTING READY

Talk about estimating and explain that when a person makes an estimate, he or she is taking a guess based on things he already knows and things he sees. Practice estimating. Ask children to guess, without counting, how many people there are in the room. Write down their estimates, and then count to see how many people there are. You can also try estimating how many blocks tall a table is or how many seeds are in a piece of fruit.

BEGIN

Show children the jar filled with beans. Ask them to guess how many beans are in it. Write each child's estimate on a slip of paper and give it to him to hold. Then, together, count out the beans into groups of ten and place the groups in paper cups. Show children how to count the contents of the cups to get the total amount. Write the total and ask children to compare it with their estimates. You can use numbers, tally marks, or a series of dots to write the estimates. Give children time to discuss and use a variety of techniques.

Pan-Balance Estimates

Demonstrate how the scale works by using familiar objects to find similar weights. Then put a pencil on one side of the scale and ask children to guess (or estimate) how many beans it will take to balance the scale with the pencil on it. Help them slowly add beans until the scale is balanced. Ask, "What else can we weigh with beans? Do you think this new object will weigh more or less beans than the pencil?"

Play a Counting Game!

Place a large pile of beans in the middle of the table and give each child a paper cup. Explain to children that they will be using the beans to play a counting game. To play, ask each child to roll the die and take the number of beans from the pile that appears on the die. Children can store their beans in their cups. After each child has had a number of turns, change the rules. Ask children to roll the die and put back the number of beans shown on the die. Continue taking turns until all the cups are empty.

Remember

▪ Make it clear to children that you welcome all of their estimates by emphasizing the process, not "right answers." One way to do this is to avoid listing children's names with their estimates.

BOOKS

These books will add to your discussions about counting and estimating.

▪ *Anno's Counting House* by Mitsumasa Anno (Putnam Publishing Group)

▪ *Count and See* by Tana Hoban (Macmillan)

▪ *One More and One Less* by Guilio Maestro (Crown)

MATH

Swings, flowers, seesaws, trees — how many do we have of these?

TAKE MATH TO THE PLAYGROUND

Aim: Children will use comparative language as they chart and graph the items on their playground.
Group size: Four to six children.
Materials: Ten each of four different stickers (simple dots or circles in different colors work best); a large piece of oaktag paper divided into four columns and covered with clear adhesive paper; clear tape; and a permanent black marker.

GETTING READY

Bring the laminated oaktag and stickers outside. Gather a few children together on the playground and invite them to look around and name some of the things they see. Use the marker to record four items the children name, such as a slide, swings, trees, and sand buckets. Invite children to draw a picture next to your words.

BEGIN

Point to each column on the oaktag and, together, name the four items again. Say, "I wonder how many of these things we have on the playground. How many do you think?" Encourage children to predict how many there are of each item. Then say, "Let's take a walk and find out! Which thing should we count first?"

Bring along one type of sticker, perhaps blue circles, to use as counters. As children find the items they chose to count first — trees, for example — invite them to place one sticker on each. Once every tree is marked with a blue sticker, search for the item in the next column. Bring a different type of sticker — maybe orange circles — and invite children to put one on each of these items. Continue until you have found and marked every category on your oaktag, each time using a different type of sticker.

Hold up the oaktag and, again, point to the first column. Say, "Now we can use the stickers to help us count. We put blue stickers on all the trees on our playground. Let's bring them back here and put them in the tree column on the oaktag. Then we'll count how many we have." As children bring stickers back, encourage them to place them in the tree column. Repeat the process for the remaining three items.

When you are finished, count the stickers in each column together. Remind children what item each color sticker stands for, then invite them to make comparisons. Are there more trees or swings? More shovels or trees? What else do children notice?

Remember
■ Children learn graphing by beginning with real objects and moving on to using symbols. You could repeat this activity and make it more challenging — instead of stickers, help children make tally marks with a pad and pencil to count objects on the playground.
■ Have clear tape available in case stickers don't stick to particular objects or to the paper after being on a tree (shovel, slide, etc.).

BOOKS

| Here are some fun counting books to share. | ■ *My Red Umbrella* by Robert Bright (William Morrow & Co.) | ■ *Count and See* by Tana Hoban (Macmillan) | ■ *Over in the Meadow* by Ezra Jack Keats (Four Winds Press) |

MATH

Bead bracelets are fun to make and match!

MATCHMAKER

Aim: Children will use matching and patterning skills and practice fine-motor skills, eye-hand coordination, and left-to-right progression as they make and match bead bracelets.

Group size: One or two children.

Materials: A three-foot by three-foot pegboard with approximately ten hooks; tape; twenty 10-inch pieces of string; large wooden stringing beads; three-by-five index cards; and colored markers.

In Advance: Set up your pegboard so the 10 hooks are evenly spaced. Next, take out 10 index cards and draw a large oval shape on each that will represent the piece of string tied into a bracelet. Draw or trace four, five, or six beads of various shapes on each "string" and put the cards aside. Take out actual pieces of the string and invite children to help you tape one end of each to make them easier to use for stringing. Tie knots on the other ends. Place the strings next to your stringing beads in the math-manipulatives area so children can play with them independently.

GETTING READY

When you notice children playing with the strings and beads, help expand their play by suggesting that they make bracelets. Help them thread four to six beads on each string and tie around their wrists. Later, put the beads away in a basket.

Another time, put the beads and strings out on a table with the pre-made index cards. Invite children to look at the shapes of the beads and the shapes on the cards and try to string their beads in the same order. (You can make these into bracelets, too.) Collect these in a basket. Then ask children to choose the markers that match the colors of the beads on their bracelets. Help them color the index-card beads to match the beads on the bracelet they have chosen. As children finish coloring, tape each card under a peg on the pegboard.

BEGIN

Bring the pegboard with index cards attached and the bracelets to circle time. Stand or lean the board next to you, within children's reach. Place the basket of bead bracelets on the floor in front of the board. Invite children to choose a bracelet and help them name the colors they see. You might say, "That's right, this bracelet has one red bead, one yellow bead, and then two more red beads." Encourage children to find the same bracelet on an

index card and hang it on the hook above that card. Repeat until all the bracelets are hanging.

Place the pegboard and basket of bracelets in your math-manipulatives area for children to use independently.

Remember
- Fives often know the names of many colors. However, begin with a couple of primary-colored beads — red and blue — and then add more colors such as yellow, green, and orange.
- Encourage children who do not know the names of colors to match the beads to the drawings.
- Many five-year-olds are beginning to count. These children might enjoy the challenge of using all the same beads on a bracelet and matching their bracelet to an index card that has the same number of beads.

BOOKS
Share these books about shape and form.

- *A Kiss Is Round* by Blossom Budney (Lothrop, Lee & Shepard)

- *Shapes, Shapes, Shapes* by Tana Hoban (Greenwillow Books)

- *The Wing on a Flea* by Ed Emberley (Little, Brown)

MATH

These activities will help fives gain a better understanding of how time is used.

EXPERIMENTING WITH TIME

Aim: Children will observe, estimate, and record temporal events.

Group size: Four or five children.

Materials: A variety of timers (windup kitchen timers, egg timers, and sand timers); experience chart paper; drawing paper; markers; and materials to make a group sand timer, such as a large jar, paper cups, and fine, clean sand.

GETTING READY

Talk with children about time. Ask, "Can people see time? How do people know what time it is?" Discuss how some things show us that time is passing, like clocks, and how we can also see the effect time has on things. Ask, "What would people do if there were no clocks?" Some children may know what time is by events at home or at school, or even the shows on television. What else helps us tell time?

BEGIN

Present the different timers. Talk about each one and the different ways timers work. Help children compare the timers. Set two timers to go off in one minute, and see if they both go off at the same time.

Help children make time estimations. For example: "How many times can you jump up and down before the sand in this timer runs out?" or "How many plastic-foam balls can you put in a box before the bell rings?" Record children's estimations on a chart and test them out together.

Help children understand that timers can also be used to measure how long it takes to do something. Ask children to choose a timer and measure how long it takes to build a block tower, paint a picture, sing a song, play a board game, etc. Which activities in your day seem to take the longest? The shortest? Help children order a few activities by time.

Make a Group Timer

Make a group sand timer by taping a paper cup with one hole in it inside a glass jar. Children can observe the timer and watch time pass in a concrete way as the sand piles up. Ask, "What would happen if we made more holes in the cup? Will the sand come out faster or slower?" Test children's ideas. Use a timer to help you place enough sand in the cup to make it last exactly one minute, two minutes, or three minutes. Try using this to time your next cleanup!

Remember:

- Help children understand that it isn't important to hurry when they time themselves. The idea is just to see how long each activity takes.

BOOKS

These books can help introduce the concept of time and clocks.

- *All Kinds of Time* by Harry Behn (Harcourt Brace Jovanovich)

- *Clocks* by Tony Barrs (Grossett & Dunlap)

- *It's About Time* by Miriam Schlein (Addison-Wesley)

ACTIVITY PLAN INDEX:
TWOS AND THREES

DEVELOPMENTAL AREAS AND SKILLS ENHANCED	MATH SKILLS									OTHER SKILLS		
	Patterning	Sorting/Classifying	Ordering/Seriating	Matching/Correspondence	Counting/Number Concepts	Measuring/Estimating	Visual/Spatial Skills	Problem Solving	Creative Thinking	Sharing/Cooperating	Language Development	Fine/Gross Motor Skills
2'S ACTIVITY PLANS												
BIG AND LITTLE, HEAVY AND LIGHT **PAGE 38**		■				■					■	■
FUN WITH BALLS AND BOXES **PAGE 39**							■	■		■	■	■
OUTDOOR PICTURE MATCH **PAGE 40**				■			■	■		■	■	■
CAN YOU TOP THIS? **PAGE 41**				■		■					■	■
EGG-CITING POMPON MATCH **PAGE 42**	■	■		■					■		■	■
ROUND AND ROUND **PAGE 43**							■	■	■			■
SMALL, MEDIUM, LARGE **PAGE 44**		■	■	■	■				■		■	
EMPTYING AND FILLING **PAGE 45**						■	■	■			■	■
SORTING WITH "BLOCK" BOXES **PAGE 46**	■	■	■						■		■	■
WHAT CAN WE DO? **PAGE 47**				■				■	■	■	■	
3'S ACTIVITY PLANS												
LET'S MAKE A GRAPH **PAGE 48**		■		■	■	■			■		■	
GRAPHING WITH PICTURE CUBES **PAGE 49**				■	■				■	■	■	■
MATCHING CONTAINERS AND LIDS **PAGE 50**				■	■	■	■				■	■
BIGGER THAN A BREAD BOX **PAGE 51**		■				■	■	■			■	■
FRUIT-KEBAB PATTERNS **PAGE 52**	■			■	■					■	■	■
SORTING AND CLASSIFYING OUTDOORS **PAGE 53**		■	■	■					■	■	■	
CRISPY CRACKER MATCH **PAGE 54**		■		■	■		■			■	■	■
LET'S PLAY MUSICAL SHAPES **PAGE 55**							■			■	■	■
LOOK AGAIN! **PAGE 56**				■	■						■	■
IF THE SHOE FITS — PUT IT IN! **PAGE 57**				■	■	■	■	■			■	■

ACTIVITY PLAN INDEX:
FOURS AND FIVES

DEVELOPMENTAL AREAS AND SKILLS ENHANCED	MATH SKILLS								OTHER SKILLS			
	Patterning	Sorting/Classifying	Ordering/Seriating	Matching/Correspondence	Counting/Number Concepts	Measuring/Estimating	Visual/Spatial Skills	Problem Solving	Creative Thinking	Sharing/Cooperating	Language Development	Fine/Gross Motor Skills
4'S ACTIVITY PLANS												
PATTERNS ARE EVERYWHERE! PAGE 58	■						■		■		■	■
MOVING PATTERNS PAGE 59	■						■		■		■	■
LET'S GO ON A MEASURING TREASURE HUNT PAGE 60			■	■		■					■	■
I KNOW WHERE IT IS! PAGE 61		■		■	■						■	■
NATURE SORTING PAGE 62		■			■				■	■	■	■
AS BIG AS ME! PAGE 63		■	■		■			■		■	■	■
KEEPING YOUR BALANCE PAGE 64						■		■	■	■	■	■
VEHICLE GRAPHING PAGE 65				■	■				■	■	■	■
HOW BIG IS BIGGEST? PAGE 66			■				■	■		■	■	
HOW MUCH IS THERE? PAGE 67				■	■	■			■	■	■	
5'S ACTIVITY PLANS												
"ME" MEASURING PAGE 68			■	■	■	■				■	■	
FILL 'ER UP! PAGE 69					■	■	■			■	■	
CLEANUP-TIME SORTING, PART I PAGE 70		■			■			■	■	■	■	■
CLEANUP-TIME SORTING, PART II PAGE 71		■		■	■			■	■	■	■	■
CIRCLES AND SQUARES AROUND US PAGE 72		■		■	■		■		■	■	■	■
SHADOW PLAY PAGE 73			■				■	■	■	■	■	
WHO'S GOT THE BEANS? PAGE 74				■	■			■		■	■	
TAKE MATH TO THE PLAYGROUND PAGE 75		■		■	■					■	■	
MATCHMAKER PAGE 76	■			■	■		■				■	■
EXPERIMENTING WITH TIME PAGE 77			■					■	■	■	■	

RESOURCES

ooking for more helpful resources on understanding and enhancing young children's math learning? Here's a sampling of recommended professional books, as well as articles to review. Check a good-sized bookstore for the titles, or order directly from the publishers. A college or university library in your area may also carry these books and magazines as part of its collection.

BOOKS

▼ *Engaging Children's Minds: The Project Approach* by Lilian G. Katz and Sylvia C. Chard (Ablex Publishing Corporation)

▼ *Explorations for Early Childhood* by Lalie Harcourt (Addison-Wesley)

▼ "Helping Young Children Learn," Chapter 8, *Mathematical, Geometric, and Spatial Reasoning* (fifth edition), by Evelyn G. Pitcher, Sylvia G. Feinburg, and David A. Alexander (Merrill, an imprint of Macmillan Publishing Company)

▼ *Mathematics Children Use and Understand: Preschool Through Third Grade* by Wilbur Dutton and Ann Dutton (Mayfield Publishing Company)

▼ *Mathematics for Every Young Child* by Karen Schultz, Ron Colaruso, and Virginia Strawderman (Merrill)

▼ *Mathematics Is More Than Counting* by Kristina Leeb-Lundberg (Association for Childhood Education International)

▼ *Mathematics Their Way: An Activity-Centered Mathematics Program for Early Childhood Education* by Mary Baratta-Lorton (Addison-Wesley)

▼ *Number in Preschool and Kindergarten: Educational Implications of Piaget's Theory* by Constance Kamii (National Association for the Education of Young Children)

ARTICLES

▼ "Discovering Math," Scholastic *Pre-K Today*, February 1992

▼ "Let's Take Math Outdoors!" by Sandra Waite-Stupiansky and Nicholas Stupiansky, Scholastic *Pre-K Today*, April 1990

▼ "Make It a Math Experience!" by Ellen Booth Church, Scholastic *Pre-K Today*, Circle Time, April 1991

▼ "Manipulatives" by Lisa Feeney, Scholastic *Pre-K Today*, Learning Through Play Family Sharing Page, April 1991

▼ "Measuring, Graphing & Estimating," by Ellen Booth Church, Scholastic *Pre-K Today*, Group Time, February 1992

▼ "Solving Problems Together!" Scholastic *Pre-K Today*, March 1991

▼ "What Can You Do?" by Ellen Booth Church, Scholastic *Pre-K Today*, Circle Time, March 1991